FLOORED!

FLOORED!

How a Misguided Fed Experiment
Deepened and Prolonged
the Great Recession

GEORGE SELGIN

CATO
INSTITUTE
WASHINGTON, D.C.

ISBN: 978-1-948647-08-3
eISBN: 978-1-948647-09-0

Jacket design: Peter Selgin and Lydia Mashburn.
Cover art: *Nude Descending a Staircase*, 1912, by Marcel Duchamp.

Library of Congress Cataloging-in-Publication Data available.

To Peter,
my better whole

CONTENTS

LIST OF FIGURES

ABBREVIATIONS

BHC: Bank Holding Company
BOJ: Bank of Japan
CDs: Certificates of Deposit
ECB: European Central Bank
FDIC: Federal Deposit Insurance Corporation
HQLA: High-Quality Liquid Asset
IOER: interest on excess reserves
LCR: Liquidity Coverage Ratio
LSAPs: large-scale asset purchases
MBS: mortgage-backed securities
NIM: net interest margin
NIRP: negative interest-rate policy
ON-RRP: overnight reverse repurchase agreement
QE: quantitative easing
SOMA: System Open Market Account

ACKNOWLEDGEMENTS

The germ of this book consists of written testimony I submitted to the House Committee on Financial Services Monetary Policy and Trade Subcommittee for its July 20, 2017, hearing on "Monetary Policy v. Fiscal Policy: Risks to Price Stability and the Economy." I therefore owe a debt of gratitude to the members of that subcommittee, especially to its chair, Congressman Andy Barr of Kentucky, for soliciting that testimony, as well as to Dino Falaschetti, the Committee's Chief Economist, for encouraging them to do so.

I'm grateful to many other persons for their help in preparing the book itself. David Beckworth, Jim Dorn, Donald Dutkowsky, Joe Gagnon, Charles Goodhart, David Laidler, Norbert Michel, Alex Pollock, Alex Shibuola, David VanHoose, and Stephen Williamson offered helpful criticisms of various versions of the manuscript. Tyler Whirty contributed invaluable research assistance; Melina Yingling prepared the figures and charts; Peter Selgin supplied the lovely cover art; and Eleanor O'Connor oversaw the publication process. Last, but most rather than least, Lydia Mashburn, the CMFA's Managing Director, assisted in virtually every stage of the project, from helping me to prepare the final draft of my Congressional testimony to proofreading the book galleys. If only I could have help like that with every book I write!

George Selgin
Washington, D.C.
June 2018

1

INTRODUCTION:
AN EXPERIMENT GONE AWRY

Federal Reserve authorities responded to the 2007–08 financial crisis with a sequence of controversial monetary policy experiments aimed at containing the crisis and, later on, at promoting recovery. One of those experiments consisted of the Fed's decision to start paying interest on depository institutions' balances with it, including both their legally required balances and any balances they held in excess of legal requirements. Because the interest rate on excess reserves was high relative to short-term market rates, the new policy led to the establishment of a "floor"-type operating system, meaning one in which changes in the rate of interest paid on excess reserves, rather than open market operations, became the Fed's chief instrument of monetary control.

Although it has attracted less attention, and generated less controversy, than many of the Fed's other crisis-related innovations, the Fed's shift to a floor system has also had more profound and enduring consequences than many of them. And despite Fed officials' intentions, those consequences, including a radical change in the Fed's methods of monetary control, have mostly been regrettable. While Fed officials hoped that the new floor system would assist them in regulating the flow of private credit in the face of extremely low and falling interest rates, a close look

at the workings of the system, and at its record, shows that those
hopes have been disappointed.

As the following pages will show, among its other consequences, the Fed's new operating system

- intensified an already severe economic downturn by
  serving as the means by which it maintained an excessively tight monetary policy;
- led to a sustained collapse in the interbank market for
  federal funds, thereby undermining the Fed's traditional
  means of monetary control, curtailing an important
  source of bank liquidity, and discouraging interbank
  monitoring;
- dramatically reduced the effectiveness of open market
  operations, so that even massive Fed asset purchases might
  not supply the stimulus to investment and spending that
  much smaller purchases would once have achieved;
- undermined productive investment by substantially
  increasing the Fed's role in allocating scarce credit; and
- increased the risk of the Fed's being called upon to undertake and finance strictly fiscal policy undertakings by sev-
  ering the traditional link between the size of its balance
  sheet and the stance of monetary policy.

In 2015 the Federal Open Market Committee (FOMC), the
Fed's monetary policy setting body, announced that it would
"begin an extended effort to evaluate potential long-run monetary policy implementation frameworks," and that the effort was
"expected to run through the end of 2016" (Board of Governors 2015). If such an evaluation ever took place, and Fed officials
arrived at some conclusions based on it, they have yet to announce
those conclusions. But it's clear that, despite having finally
embarked upon a program of monetary policy "normalization"

involving the gradual lifting of its policy rates and a reduction in the size of its balance sheet, many top Fed officials appear to be strongly inclined to make the current floor system permanent.

Notwithstanding that inclination, Fed officials say that they're still willing to entertain the possibility of switching from the current system to a more conventional "corridor"-type system. This book's purpose is to encourage them in that direction, while also making others aware of the present system's shortcomings. It will explain in detail how the Fed's floor-system experiment came about, what its intended and actual consequences have been, and why either the Fed itself or Congress should bring the experiment to an end as rapidly as can be done without causing any further, avoidable economic damage.

2

PRELUDE: MONETARY CONTROL
BEFORE THE CRISIS

To appreciate the radical changes made to the Fed's operating system during the financial crisis, it's helpful to first review how the Fed managed monetary policy before then, and particularly during the period known as the "Great Moderation"—a time of modest and stable inflation and otherwise relatively low macroeconomic volatility that began in the mid-1980s and ended when the crisis struck.

Targeting the Fed Funds Rate

It happens that the Great Moderation period almost perfectly coincided with the FOMC's decision, following Fed Chair Paul Volcker's successful taming of the Great Inflation of the 1970s, to implement monetary policy by setting an explicit target for the federal funds rate, the overnight interest rate at which institutions that keep deposit balances at the Fed lend those balances to, or borrow them from, other such institutions. The fed funds market served in those days mainly as a means by which banks in danger of falling short of their minimum reserve requirements could make up for reserve shortages by borrowing from banks with reserves to spare.[1] Because bank reserves didn't bear any interest, and the fed funds rate was always positive, banks with surplus or "excess" reserves were always happy to lend those reserves overnight. Thanks to the fed funds market, banks could collectively make do with very few excess reserves, knowing that interbank lending would place available reserves wherever they were needed.

Back then, as ever since, the Fed operated under the so-called "dual mandate"—the requirement, first incorporated into the Federal Reserve Act in 1977, that the Fed manage monetary policy so as to "promote effectively the goals of maximum employment, stable prices, and moderate long-term interest rates." Under the fed funds rate-targeting regime, the Fed faced a twofold challenge. First, it had to choose a fed funds rate target that it hoped would prove consistent with fulfilling the dual mandate, meaning a target that would be low enough to guard against excessive unemployment but high enough to keep inflation under control. Then it had to manage the supply of bank reserves to keep the actual federal funds rate at its targeted level.

The details concerning just how the FOMC decided where to set its fed funds target need not concern us. Instead, we may simply observe that although the FOMC's choices were supported by rafts of statistics and elaborate forecasts based on them, they also involved a measure of trial and error. If, for example, the FOMC believed that the Fed's policy stance was likely to result in an unwanted decline in inflation, increased unemployment, or a combination of both, it would adopt a looser stance. That would mean lowering its fed funds rate target, which in turn would mean a loosened market for bank reserves and a general inclination for banks to ease their own lending terms. If, on the other hand, the

---

[1] Although the Fed allows banks to overdraw their accounts during the day, it requires them to end each day with non-zero balances sufficient to meet their reserve requirements, or else pay a penalty.

likely course of inflation, unemployment, or both suggested the need for a tighter policy stance, the FOMC would raise its fed funds rate target, encouraging banks to tighten in turn.

Although the FOMC never relied on any simple algorithm to determine its rate target, John Taylor (1993) found that its rate settings during much of the Great Moderation period[2] could be approximated by the simple formula, now known as the "Taylor Rule,"

$$FFR^* = 2 + \pi_t + .5(\pi_t - \pi^*) + .5(y_t - y_t^*),$$

where FFR^* is the chosen rate target; 2 is the assumed, constant long-run value of the real (inflation-adjusted) fed funds rate; π_t and π^* are the actual and target inflation rate; and y_t and y_t^* are actual and "potential" (that is, "maximum employment") levels of output.

Open Market Operations

It's important to note that the federal funds rate, whose value the FOMC endeavors to control, is a private-market rate. Its level, like those of other market-determined interest rates, depends on the interaction of supply and demand—specifically, the supply of and demand for reserve balances at the Fed, a.k.a. "federal funds."

Because the Fed did not yet pay interest on reserve balances banks kept with it, the only direct influence it had on banks' demand for federal funds was through its setting of minimum reserve requirements. While these requirements were occasionally adjusted over the course of the Great Moderation, the adjustments were aimed not at influencing the stance of monetary policy but at relaxing the burden reserve requirements placed on banks subject

---

[2] Taylor (2009, Chapter 1) claims that the Fed's policy stance after the dot-com crash of 2001 was easier than what the Taylor Rule would have prescribed, and that by departing from that rule, the Fed inadvertently contributed to the subprime boom and bust.

to them (Feinman 1993). As far as the Fed's day-to-day operations were concerned, monetary control was a matter of adjusting the *supply* of federal funds to make the funds rate land on target.

To do that, the Fed relied upon "Open Market Operations," meaning purchases or sales of government securities, and short-term Treasury securities especially, from a score or so of approved ("primary") security dealers. To add to the supply of federal funds and thereby put downward pressure on the fed funds rate, the Fed would buy securities; to reduce the supply, it would sell securities in its possession. The operations were handled by the New York Fed's Open Market Trading Desk and supervised by the FOMC-appointed manager of its System Open Market Account (SOMA). The Desk would arrange the necessary auctions, which were usually held daily, based on estimates of the direction and scope of the operations needed to move the funds rate to its target, or to keep it from moving away from it.

How did open market operations alter the supply of federal funds? When the Fed bought securities, it paid dealers who made the sales by crediting the dealers' own Fed deposit balances (if the dealers were themselves banks) or by crediting the balances of the dealers' banks, and so increased the total supply of federal funds by the amount of the purchase. When it sold securities, it debited dealer and dealer-affiliated reserve balances by the amount of their successful bids, reducing the total quantity of outstanding federal funds by the same amount.

Because keeping the actual fed funds rate near its target often meant adjusting the supply of reserves to meet temporary rather than persistent changes in the demand for them, the Fed undertook both "permanent" and "temporary" open market operations. Permanent operations involve "outright" security purchases or (more rarely) sales, whereas temporary ones involve purchases or sales accompanied by "repurchase agreements," or "repos." (For convenience, the term "repo" is in practice used to describe a complete sale and repurchase transaction.) For example, the Fed might purchase securities from dealers on the condition that they agreed to repurchase those securities a day later, thereby increasing the supply of reserves for a single night only. (The opposite operation, where the Fed sells securities with the understanding that it will buy them back the next day, is called an "overnight reverse repo.") Practically speaking, repos are collateralized loans, except in name, where the securities being purchased are the loan collateral and the difference between their purchase and repurchase price constitutes the return on the loan. Expressed in annual percentage terms, that return is known as the "repo rate." The obvious advantage of repos, and shorter-term repos especially, is that, because they are self-reversing, a central bank that relies extensively on them can for the most part avoid resorting to open market sales when it wishes to reduce the supply of federal funds. Instead, it merely has to refrain from "rolling over" or otherwise replacing some of its maturing repos.

The Monetary "Transmission Mechanism"

Although the immediate goal of the Fed's open market operations was to keep the federal funds rate on target, their ultimate purpose was achieving a monetary policy stance consistent with the Fed's dual mandate. As we've seen, the Taylor Rule supplies a rough indication of how the Fed adjusted its fed funds rate target in response to actual and desired levels of inflation and output. The Great Moderation suggests, furthermore, that by setting its fed funds targets as if it were heeding that rule, the Fed was in fact able to keep actual inflation and output from veering far from their desired levels.

The causal chain connecting the Fed's rate-targeting procedures and its ultimate policy objectives is sometimes referred to as the "monetary transmission mechanism." To consider a very simple case, albeit one that's especially pertinent to our subject, suppose that, at its current rate setting, the FOMC anticipates below target inflation and unemployment. Consequently, it reduces its fed funds rate target while instructing the SOMA account manager to arrange open market security purchases sufficient to drive the actual funds rate down to its reduced target level. The purchases—say $20 billion—increase banks' reserve balances by a like amount. Assuming that banks had been meeting their reserve requirements, the banks find themselves collectively holding $20 billion in excess reserves. Because bank reserves earn no interest, they'll seek to dispose of the excess, initially by increasing their offers of fed funds. That in turn pushes the fed funds rate down, helping the Fed to hit its lowered target.

But that's not the whole story, because lending on the fed funds market only shifts excess reserves around, without reducing their total quantity. As banks (again, collectively) find themselves confronted with a persistent reserve surplus, they'll engage in other sorts of lending, including retail lending, that involves crediting borrowers' deposit accounts. Such lending will continue until bank deposits have grown enough to transform the former excess reserves into required reserves, achieving a full equilibrium of reserve supply and demand. The expansion of bank loans and deposits, each by some multiple of the new reserves, contributes to a like expansion of overall total spending in the economy, which puts upward pressure on prices (or at least combats any tendency for them to decline) while reducing slack in the labor market. Thus, besides serving to keep the fed funds rate on target, the Fed's open market operations ultimately serve to keep inflation and employment themselves at desired levels.

★★★

Such, in a nutshell, was monetary control prior to the financial crisis. The rest of this book is about how a seemingly minor change in Fed policy overturned its traditional system of monetary control, replacing it with one that was radically different—and, in several important respects, inferior.

3

INTEREST ON BANK RESERVES

Economists have long understood that, so long as bank reserves bear no interest, minimum reserve requirements, whether they're met using banks' holdings of vault cash or with central bank deposit balances, act like a tax on bank deposits and therefore on bank depositors.[3] Although the Fed earns interest on the assets backing banks' reserves, until October 2008 it didn't share that interest with commercial banks. Instead, it remitted all its interest earnings, net of its operating expenses, to the U.S. Treasury.

Though it was only in the midst of the recent financial crisis that the Fed first began paying interest on bank reserves, the possibility of its doing so has long been a subject of discussion and debate. Indeed, the idea was initially broached during the discussions that led to the passage of the original Federal Reserve Act in 1913. That original suggestion was ultimately rejected, in large part because of opposition from Wall Street banks, which saw it as a threat to their lucrative correspondent business.[4]

So matters stood for more than half a century, thanks to the generally low inflation and interest-rate environment that

---

[3] See, for example, Feinman (1993).
[4] On Wall Street banks' role in shaping the Federal Reserve Act, see Selgin (2016).

prevailed during most of that time, and, after 1933, to the fact that Regulation Q and other provisions of the 1933 Banking Act relieved commercial banks themselves of pressure to pay competitive rates of interest on their own deposit balances.

Starting in the mid-1960s, however, a combination of rising inflation, declining Fed membership, the rise of Money Market Mutual Funds, and increasingly intense global banking competition, revived Fed officials' desire to be able to pay interest on bank reserves: because they regarded mandatory reserve requirements as an aid to monetary control, Fed officials preferred this alternative to that of dispensing with reserve requirements altogether (see Weiner 1985; Higgins 1977; and Eubanks 2002). Over the course of the next several decades, Fed officials tried several times to gain Congress's permission to pay interest on reserves.[5] Until 2006 these attempts were successfully opposed by the U.S. Treasury, which feared having its seigniorage earnings substantially reduced. But in that year, the Fed finally managed to have the authority it had long sought included among the provisions of the Financial Services Regulatory Relief Act.

The Fed's ultimate success was made possible in large part by reduced Treasury opposition, which itself came about as a result of a considerable decline, during the 1990s, in the amount of seignorage revenue reserve requirements were generating. Although required reserve ratios were reduced somewhat during that time, the main cause of the decline in revenue was banks' successful

---

[5] As Goodfriend and Hargraves (1983, pp. 16–17) report, in 1978 the Fed went so far as to declare that, because statute law didn't expressly prohibit it from doing so, it planned to start paying interest on reserves without Congress's permission. That gambit came to grief when Representative Henry Reuss and Senator William Proxmire, the chairmen of the House and Senate Banking Committees, respectively, called it "a blatant usurpation of Congressional powers [that] would raise profound questions about the continued independence of the Fed."

use of "sweep accounts" to avoid the requirements.[6] By substantially reducing the effective reserve tax base, sweep accounts also reduced the cost to the Treasury of allowing the Fed to pay interest on reserves: the effect of this further innovation on its earnings was no longer as substantial as it might have been in the past.

By the same token, however, the reduced burden of reserve requirements also limited the "regulatory relief" banks would gain from interest payments on reserves. Perhaps in recognition of this, Fed officials, in making their successful bid for the right to pay interest on bank reserves, offered new grounds for doing so that had nothing to do with reducing the reserve tax. In particular, then Fed Governor Donald Kohn (2005) argued that, besides making it unnecessary for banks to resort to sweep accounts and other "reserve avoidance measures," paying interest on reserves would assist the Fed in conducting monetary policy "by establishing a sufficient and predictable demand for balances at the Reserve Banks so that the System knows the volume of reserves to supply (or remove) through open market operations to achieve the FOMC's target federal funds rate."

Importantly, in view of later developments, Kohn's statement implied that interest on reserves was meant to support rather than supplant the Fed's traditional methods of monetary control, including its reliance upon open market operations as its chief tool for reaching its monetary targets. Interest on reserves, Kohn said,

> Would act as a *minimum* for overnight interest rates, because banks would not generally lend to other banks at a lower rate than they could earn by keeping their excess funds at a

---

[6] Sweep accounts are pairs of accounts set up for the same account balance so that funds can be shifted or "swept" automatically from one account to the other. To avoid reserve requirements, during overnight reserve monitoring periods banks "sweep" customers' balances from accounts subject to such requirements, such as checking accounts, into exempt ones, such as money market accounts.

Reserve Bank. Although the Board sees no need to pay interest on excess reserves in the near future, and any movement in this direction would need further study, the ability to do so would be a potentially useful addition to the monetary toolkit of the Federal Reserve (ibid; emphasis added).

By recommending that the Fed set aside the possibility of paying interest on *excess* reserves for "further study," Kohn made it clear that his own case for paying interest on reserves was one for paying interest on *required* reserves only. As events would show, paying interest on excess reserves (IOER) could actually undermine both efficiency and monetary control by causing banks to accumulate unlimited quantities of such reserves.

Kohn's remarks also make it clear that, far from even entertaining a radical change in its operating system, the Fed was merely toying with the possibility of eventually paying interest on banks' excess reserve balances for the purpose of establishing an orthodox "corridor" system of the sort that several other central banks were then employing. In an orthodox corridor system, a variable but generally positive interest rate on bank reserves, rather than a zero rate, serves as a lower bound for the central bank's policy rate, while the central bank's emergency lending rate serves as an upper bound. Although the policy rate can vary within these limits, it generally stays close to a target set, in the most common "symmetrical" corridor arrangements, halfway between them.[7] To keep the overnight rate on target, the central bank relies on a combination of open market operations and changes to the administered rates that define the corridor's lower and upper

---

[7] Before 2008, symmetrical corridor systems with positive deposit rates were employed by the European Central Bank (ECB), the Bank of England, the Riksbank, the Bank of Canada, the Reserve Bank of Australia, and the Reserve Bank of New Zealand, among other central banks. Norges Bank maintained an asymmetrical corridor.

bounds, where open market operations alter the supply of, and the administered rate settings the demand for, overnight funds. Except on those infrequent occasions when either of the corridor's limits becomes binding, open market operations continue to be an effective means for maintaining the central bank's monetary policy stance, especially by serving to dampen overnight rate fluctuations within the corridor (Kahn 2010, pp. 13–15). For that reason, a switch to a corridor system would not have involved any radical change in the Fed's monetary control procedures.

Indeed, the Fed's "Great Moderation" operating system, discussed earlier, might be described as a corridor system of sorts, albeit one that involved an asymmetrical and variable corridor based on a zero IOER rate and a discount ("primary credit") rate set at a fixed spread above the federal funds rate target.[8] As we've seen, in that regime the Fed relied on open market operations to achieve its policy target. Had the Fed employed interest on reserves to establish a proper corridor system, as it planned to do in 2006, and even had it allowed interest to be paid on excess reserves with that aim alone in mind, paying interest on reserves wouldn't have constituted a radical change. But as we shall see, when the Fed finally put its new tool to work, a corridor system was no longer what it had in mind.

---

[8] The primary credit–fed funds target rate spread, which was set at 100 basis points from January 9, 2003, until August 17, 2007, was halved on the latter date, and halved again, to just 25 basis points, on March 16, 2008. On February 19, 2010, the spread was returned to 50 basis points, where it has since remained.

4

THE FLOOR SYSTEM'S BEGINNINGS

Fear of Falling

The 2006 Financial Services Regulatory Relief Act would have allowed the Fed to begin paying interest on depository institutions' reserve balances commencing October 1, 2011. However, the worsening financial crisis of 2008 led to the passage of the Emergency Economic Stabilization Act, which advanced the measure's effective date to October 1, 2008.

Fed officials sought and received Congress's authorization to begin paying interest on reserves three years ahead of schedule for a reason completely unrelated to those that Kohn and others had offered in defense of the original measure. As former Fed Chair Ben Bernanke explains in his memoir,

> We had initially asked to pay interest on reserves for technical reasons. But in 2008, we needed the authority to solve an increasingly serious problem: the risk that our emergency lending, which had the side effect of increasing bank reserves, would lead short-term interest rates to fall below our federal funds target and thereby cause us to lose control of monetary policy. When banks have lots of reserves, they have less need to borrow from each other, which pushes down the interest rate on that borrowing—the federal funds rate.

Until this point we had been selling Treasury securities we owned to offset the effect of our [emergency] lending on reserves (the process called sterilization). But as our lending increased, that stopgap response would at some point no longer be possible because we would run out of Treasuries to sell. At that point, without legislative action, we would be forced to either limit the size of our interventions . . . or lose the ability to control the federal funds rate, the main instrument of monetary policy. So, by setting the interest rate we paid on reserves *high enough*, we could prevent the federal funds rate from falling too low, *no matter how much [emergency] lending we did* (Bernanke 2015, pp. 325–26; emphasis added).

The same understanding of the Fed's intention in implementing IOER three years ahead of the original 2006 schedule was conveyed in the Board of Governors' (2008a) October 6, 2008, press release announcing the Fed's new tool:

The payment of interest on excess reserves will permit the Federal Reserve to expand its balance sheet as necessary to provide the liquidity necessary to support financial stability while implementing the monetary policy that is appropriate in light of the System's macroeconomic objectives of maximum employment and price stability.

More than a year later, with the advantage of hindsight, Richmond Fed economists John R. Walter and Renee Courtois (2009) offered an almost identical account. The Fed's emergency credit injections, they wrote,

had the potential to push the fed funds rate below its target, increasing the overall supply of credit to the economy beyond a level consistent with the Fed's macroeconomic policy goals, particularly concerning price stability. . . . Once banks began earning interest on the excess reserves they held, they would be more willing to hold on to excess reserves instead of attempting to purge them from their balance sheets.

Although their meaning may seem surprising in light of subsequent developments, these official statements, as well as many others like them, make it clear that the Fed's main concern in October 2008 was that of avoiding an unplanned *loosening* of what it still considered an appropriate monetary policy stance. Although they were keen on providing emergency support to particular firms and markets, Fed officials recognized no general liquidity shortage calling for further monetary accommodation. The challenge, as they saw it, was that of extending credit to specific recipients without promoting a general increase in lending and spending.

Figure 4.1 may further clarify the Fed's reasoning. The solid black line shows the Fed's total assets, while the solid grey line shows its Treasury holdings, before and since Lehman's failure. That failure was followed by a dramatic increase in the Fed's emergency lending. Because the Fed's Treasury holdings had already fallen by then to what Fed officials considered a minimal level, and because those officials were determined to keep the fed

Figure 4.1: Federal Reserve System Total Assets and Treasury Securities Holdings, Treasury Supplementary Financing Account

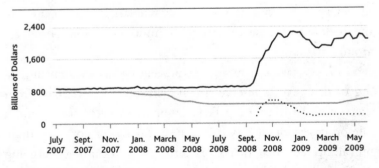

—— Federal Reserve Banks Total Assets
—— Federal Reserve Bank Holdings of U.S. Treasury Securities
···· U.S. Treasury Supplementary Financing Account

Source: Federal Reserve Bank of St. Louis FRED Database.

funds rate from falling below its target, they needed some other way to keep new reserves the Fed was creating from flooding into the fed funds market. While the Treasury, at the Fed's behest, did its part by diverting funds to a "Supplementary Finance Account" created for the express purpose of reducing banks' share of total Fed balances (dotted line), for the most part the Fed was counting on IOER to encourage banks to accumulate excess reserves instead of lending them.

From Corridor to Floor

Fed officials' desire have IOER serve as a substitute for sterilizing the Fed's emergency loans was fundamentally inconsistent with having the IOER rate serve as the lower bound of a corridor system, orthodox or otherwise. Yet that same October 2008 FOMC press release suggests that they were at first unaware of this. "The rate paid on excess balances," the release announced, "will be set initially as the lowest targeted federal funds rate for each reserve maintenance period less 75 basis points," which setting would "establish a lower bound on the federal funds rate." The intent here seemed to be that of establishing an orthodox corridor system, in which the IOER rate is typically *below* the monetary authority's intended policy rate target, with changes in the stock of bank reserves serving to limit fluctuations of the rate around that target.

But to serve as a means for preventing banks from disposing of their excess reserves in the fed funds market, and from thereby undermining the Fed's attempts to keep the fed funds rate on target, the IOER had to be as high as, if not *higher* than, prevailing rates on other short-term loans, including the going ("effective") federal funds rate. Just how an IOER rate set 75 basis points *below* "the lowest targeted federal funds rate" could do that, and specifically how it could keep the effective fed funds rate from eventually slipping as much as 75 basis points *below* the Fed's stated target, the Board's press release didn't explain. Nor could it have, since IOER could only keep the fed funds rate from falling below the Fed's target if the IOER rate was set equal to, or rather (for reasons we'll come to) above, the target. Partly for this very reason, the effective fed funds rate continued to decline.

What the Fed really needed, if it was to stick to its desired fed funds target, was not a corridor system but what Marvin Goodfriend (2002) and others have called a "floor" system. In a floor system, the IOER rate itself becomes the central bank's policy rate and chief instrument of monetary control, replacing open market operations in that role.[9] The difference between the two arrangements is illustrated in Figure 4.2.

Figure 4.2: Corridor and Floor Operating Systems

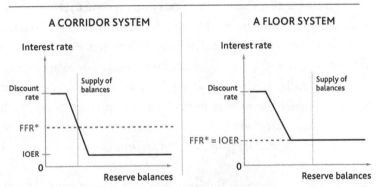

Source: Reproduced from Keister 2012.

[9] In a conference call held on September 29, 2008, or just days before the Emergency Economic Stabilization Act was passed, the FOMC, which was then planning to set the IOER rate at 50 basis points below its fed funds target, was told by Brian Madigan, the FOMC's Secretary and Director of the Fed's Division of Monetary Affairs, that the arrangement they were contemplating "may turn out [to] operate more like what we have been calling a floor system." However, Madigan added, while the FOMC might eventually "need to use the excess reserve rate as the way to effectively set the federal funds rate," it would have "to see how it goes and get some experience" (Board of Governors 2008a).

In a corridor system, as we've seen, the target fed funds rate is set between, typically half-way between, the IOER rate and the discount (or primary credit) rate, and either open market operations or changes in the interest rate on excess reserves can be employed to keep the effective funds rate close to its target value. In a floor system, in contrast, the Fed pays an IOER rate equal to its desired fed funds rate target, thereby allowing the IOER rate to serve, in Goodfriend's words, as both a "floor under which banks would not lend reserves to each other" *and* "a ceiling above which banks would not lend to each other." Because banks can earn at least as much by holding reserve balances ("federal funds") as they can by lending them, and with less effort, the demand schedule for fed funds becomes flat—that is, infinitely interest-elastic—at the IOER rate. The Fed could then maintain a desired fed funds rate target even as it flooded the market with bank reserves.

It happens that the Board's press announcement stated, conveniently, that "the formula for the interest rate on excess balances may be adjusted subsequently in light of experience and evolving market conditions." The Fed was quick to take advantage of this clause. Its initial IOER rate settings, shown in Figure 4.3, saw it stumble during the new regime's first month from its original, corridor-style rate-setting plan to a floor-system plan consistent with its goal of encouraging banks to accumulate rather than lend federal funds.

Having first set the IOER rate at 75 basis points on October 9, 2008—that is, 75 basis points below its 150-basis-point federal funds rate target, and also below the then prevailing effective federal funds rate—the Board raised it to 115 basis points on October 23, narrowing the IOER-fed funds target spread to just 35 basis points. It maintained that spread as it lowered the funds rate target to 100 basis points on October 29. But on November 6, just one month after introducing the new policy, it eliminated the spread entirely by raising the IOER rate to 100 basis points.

Figure 4.3: The IOER Rate and Effective and Target Fed Funds Rates

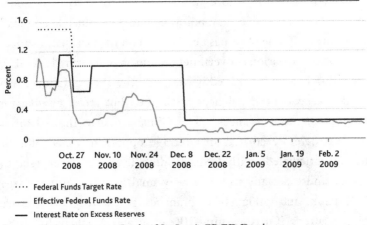

---- Federal Funds Target Rate
— Effective Federal Funds Rate
— Interest Rate on Excess Reserves

Source: Federal Reserve Bank of St. Louis FRED Database.

From then onwards, the effective fed funds rate remained persistently below the IOER rate, notwithstanding the Fed's December 17, 2008 decision to reduce the IOER rate to just 25 basis points, where it stayed for seven full years. A floor system was thus established, albeit one with some unorthodox properties.

A Floor with a Subfloor

Although the Fed's IOER adjustments achieved its immediate purpose of discouraging banks from disposing of their excess reserves in the fed funds market, those adjustments failed to achieve the Fed's ultimate goal of keeping the effective fed funds rate on target. Instead, as the Fed made its way from a corridor to a floor system, the gap between the Fed's rate target and the effective fed funds rate continued to widen. By November 6 the effective fed funds rate had plunged to just 23 basis points—far below the Fed's 100 basis point target.

That IOER failed to keep the fed funds rate on target even after the IOER rate was set equal to that target was both inconsistent with the way a floor system was supposed to work and a source of considerable disappointment to Fed officials and staff economists. Blame for it has been placed on the fact that, in addition to banks, various government-sponsored enterprises (GSEs), including Fannie Mae, Freddy Mac, and the Federal Home Loan Banks, keep deposit balances at the Fed but aren't eligible for interest on those balances.[10] The GSEs' access to the fed funds market therefore created an arbitrage opportunity Fed officials hadn't anticipated, with GSEs lending fed funds overnight to banks, and especially to a relatively small number of very large U.S. banks and foreign bank branches, in exchange for a share of the latter's IOER earnings (Keating and Machiavelli 2018). Because relatively few banks were doing most of the bidding for fed funds, they enjoyed some monopsony power (the buying side equivalent of monopoly power), and so were usually able to acquire reserves for substantially less than what they earned on them. When the IOER rate was 25 basis points, for example, one of the Federal Home Loan Banks might lend fed funds to a major commercial bank for 10 basis points, allowing the commercial bank to profit from the difference but still securing for itself a return greater than the zero rate it would earn if it just held on to its Fed balance.

Consequently, instead of getting the solid floor it wanted, the Fed had to settle for a "leaky" floor. Indeed, because the effective fed funds rate tended to fall below the IOER rate, the latter ended up looking less like a floor than like a ceiling—just the opposite of

---

[10] See Kahn (2010). The Bank of England's floor system has been leaky as well, for the similar reason that some institutions that lend in the UK's sterling overnight interbank market do not have Bank of England accounts and are therefore unable to earn the Bank Rate paid on such accounts (Bowman, Gagnon, and Leahy, pp. 3–4).

a corridor arrangement. When, in mid-December 2015, the Fed introduced a new overnight reverse repo agreement (ON-RRP) facility to create what Stephen Williamson (2016) calls a "floor-with-sub-floor" system, with the effective fed funds rate trading between the IOER rate floor and the new ON-RRP subfloor, the resemblance of the Fed's new system to a corridor system gone topsy-turvy became complete.

A Banking System Tipping Point

It can't be stressed enough that, although the interest rate paid on excess reserves seemed paltry, and especially so between December 2008 and December 2015, when it was just 25 basis points, that paltry rate was high enough compared to other lending rates—and to overnight lending rates especially—to inspire the significant changes in bank behavior. Such changes are unavoidable, if not necessarily welcome, consequences of any switch from a corridor-type to a floor-type central bank operating framework.

In particular, as David VanHoose and Donald Dutkowsky (2017) convincingly demonstrate, even at its lowest level, the Fed's IOER rate was high enough to cause banks to respond to the Fed's reserve-creating activities by accumulating excess reserves instead of taking part, as they otherwise would have, in additional wholesale lending. Using a fairly conventional bank optimization model, Dutkowsky and VanHoose first show that the model allows for four distinct equilibrium outcomes, depending on the value of various interest rate and bank resource cost parameters, and also on the banking system's required reserve ratio. These outcomes are (1) a "corridor" regime in which banks do not hold excess reserves but do engage in wholesale lending; (2) a "floor" regime in which they accumulate excess reserves but do not engage in wholesale lending; (3) a "mixed" regime in which they engage in wholesale lending but also accumulate excess reserves; and (4) a "neither" regime in which they refrain from both wholesale lending and reserve accumulation, devoting their resources exclusively to retail lending.

Dutkowsky and VanHoose show that their model's "mixed" and "neither" regime outcomes occur only for relatively few parameter combinations, with most combinations leading to either a corridor- or a floor-system outcome. Furthermore, and most importantly, they show that even very slight changes to the IOER rate can trigger a switch from a corridor to a floor regime, and they are especially likely to do so when interest rates are generally low. Finally, Dutkowsky and VanHoose test their model using calibrated values of its structural parameters for the pre- and post–October 2008 periods. They find that the model does indeed predict the regime change that occurred, so that the change can in fact be attributed to the Fed's decision to begin paying interest on bank reserves.

Figure 4.4, reproduced from Dutkowsky and VanHoose (2017, p. 11), shows the regimes that will prevail for various combinations

Figure 4.4: Corridor, Floor, and Other Regime Boundaries for Various IOER (rQ) and Wholesale Lending (rF) Rates

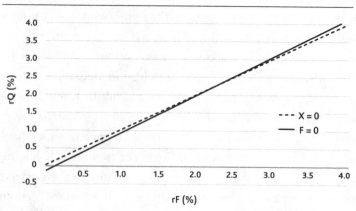

Source: Reproduced from Dutkowsky and VanHoose 2017, p. 11.

of the IOER rate (rQ) and the wholesale lending rate (rF), given other assumed parameter values, and the boundary lines separating them. For all combinations above the solid boundary line, banks refrained from wholesale lending (F = 0); for all combinations below the dashed line, they refrain from accumulating excess reserves (X = 0). The tiny slivers between the two lines contain combinations that give rise to either the "neither" (left side) or the "mixed" (right side) regime. Among other things, the figure implies that, *even had the IOER rate been left at zero, banks would not have accumulated reserves so long as the effective federal funds rate itself remained at or above 6 basis points.*

Figure 4.5, also from Dutkowsky and VanHoose, shows where the switching boundary lines shown in the previous figure stood relative to the effective federal funds rate between December 17, 2008, and December 17, 2015, when the IOER rate was fixed

Figure 4.5: Federal Funds Rate Boundary Conditions for Excess Reserve Accumulation and Wholesale Lending, and the Effective Federal Funds Rate, December 2008–December 2015

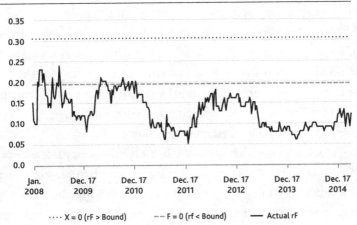

····· X = 0 (rF > Bound)   − − F = 0 (rf < Bound)   —— Actual rF

Source: Reproduced from Dutkowsky and VanHoose 2017, p. 13.

at 25 basis points. Apart from several instances (during the first half of 2009 and the second half of 2010) in which it predicts a "mixed" equilibrium, Dutkowsky and VanHoose's calibration exercise predicts that the Fed would have operated a floor system, and that it generally might have done so even had the IOER rate been considerably lower—but *not*, once again, if it had been at or only a few points above zero.

The Floor System and the Friedman Rule

What became, in this transition from a corridor to a (leaky) floor system, of the Fed's precrisis plan to use interest payments on reserves to eliminate the tax burden of reserve requirements to discourage banks from expending valuable resources on sweep accounts and other devices for avoiding such requirements?

Most writings concerning the Fed's floor system (e.g., Keister, Martin, and McAndrews 2015) seem to take for granted that the IOER rates the Fed has set in establishing and maintaining that system have been at least roughly consistent with Milton Friedman's (1969) famous rule for achieving an "Optimum Quantity of Money," according to which money balances ought to yield an average return competitive with that on other assets. Although Friedman, bearing in mind the practical impossibility of paying interest on currency, suggested that his rule might be satisfied by means of a deflation rate corresponding to the real rate of return on private financial assets, his rule can in principle also be satisfied without resorting to deflation, by having money assets, including bank reserves, bear interest.

Does it follow, then, that the Fed's IOER policy is itself optimal? It doesn't, for two reasons. First and most obvious, while there is a unique IOER rate consistent with satisfying the Friedman rule, any rate either equal to or above the Friedman-rule rate might serve to implement and maintain a floor system. In other words, although its move to a floor system meant that the Fed no longer taxed bank reserves, that move also made it possible for the Fed to *subsidize* bank reserve holding by paying a return on reserves exceeding that on other risk-free assets. We shall soon consider evidence that this has in fact been the case.[11]

Second, a return on money *below* the Friedman-rule return is likely to be optimal under many common circumstances. That can happen, for example, if other means for raising government revenue that might make up for revenues formerly generated by the reserve tax are also distortionary, or when nominal prices are inflexible or "rigid" (Phelps 1973; Walsh 1984; Schmidt-Grohé and Uribe 2004). According to a recent estimate by Matthew Canzoneri, Robert Cumby, and Behzad Diba (2016), taking account of the costliness of nominal price adjustment alone, the optimal "tax" on excess reserves, instead of being zero, would be somewhere between 20 and 40 basis points in the steady-state. For much of the postcrisis period, this would have meant paying a *negative* interest rate on banks' excess reserves, as several central banks eventually chose to do. Allowing for other externalities, or

---

[11] It is sometimes said that because reserves can be created "costlessly," there is no risk of encouraging banks to hold too many of them. But while this claim is borne out by some very simplistic models, it is never correct in practice. Even allowing that the *nominal* stock of bank reserves can be increased costlessly, the real stock can be increased only by reducing commercial banks' share in total financial intermediation relative to the share handled by the central bank. Because commercial bank assets can include loans and securities that most central banks are (for good reasons) not allowed to possess, any increase in a central bank's total intermediation share has real consequences, and those consequences are generally detrimental. Indeed, they can be so detrimental that an entire literature on "financial repression" is devoted to discussing them (Ito 2009). An ideal IOER policy must therefore steer a path between the Scylla of financial repression on the one hand and the Charybdis of suboptimal liquidity on the other. Moreover, even such an ideal policy would neither justify nor make up for the inherent inefficiency of binding minimal reserve requirements—a point often overlooked in the literature. I discuss the financially repressive consequences of the Fed's floor system in Chapter 10.

for the fact that other taxes tend to be distortionary, makes the optimal reserve tax even higher.

A Dubious Advantage

Optimal tax or not, the Fed hoped that, if its new floor system couldn't keep the effective funds rate from falling below its intended target despite a rapidly expanding Fed balance sheet, it could at least save the day by keeping that rate above its zero lower bound (Board of Governors 2008b). As I've observed elsewhere (Selgin 2017a), the logic underpinning that last hope was more than a little tortured. If there is reason to fear the zero lower bound, it's because, once the fed funds rate reaches zero, banks, instead of seeking to exchange excess reserves for other assets, will become indifferent between those alternatives. "Banks," Marvin Goodfriend (2002, p. 2) explains,

> will never lend reserves to each other at negative (nominal) interest if reserve deposits are costless to store (carry) at the central bank. The zero bound on the nominal interbank rate is a consequence of the fact that a central bank stores bank reserves for free.

At the zero lower bound, ordinary Fed rate cuts may be practically or legally impossible. Those inclined to identify monetary easing with rate cuts see this as "the" problem. But that's taking a superficial view of matters. The real problem is that, at the zero lower bound, assets that usually bear interest cease to be more attractive than money, placing the economy in a "liquidity trap." In such a trap, St. Louis Fed economists Maria Arias and Yi Wen (2014) explain,

> increases in money supply are fully absorbed by excess demand for money (liquidity); investors hoard the increased money instead of spending it because the opportunity cost of holding cash—the foregone earnings from interest—is zero when the nominal interest rate is zero.

In particular, banks will tend to hoard new reserves that come their way instead of taking advantage of them to engage in more bank lending and deposit creation. As Congressman Alan Goldsborough famously put it in 1935, in attempting to induce more bank lending by adding to the stock of bank reserves, the Fed could find itself "pushing on a string."[12]

How, then, might a *positive* IOER rate help? To be sure, it can solve the "zero lower bound problem" superficially by establishing a positive fed funds rate floor. But to what end? IOER would then render additions to the stock of bank reserves ineffective as a source of stimulus *before* the fed funds rate reached zero rather than once it did so. Yes, with the help of (positive) IOER, the Fed might set and achieve whatever positive rate target it liked, and it might do so regardless of how many reserves it created. But this "decoupling"[13] of interest rates changes from changes in the scarcity of bank reserves, applauded by Goodfriend (ibid.), Keister (2012), and Keister, Martin, and McAndrews (2008) as a feature of a floor system, might also be considered a bug: the extra freedom it entails comes at a very great price, to wit, the Fed's inability to use its reserve-creating powers to promote additional bank lending and spending.[14]

---

[12] Whether the U.S. economy was actually in a liquidity trap in the 1930s is controversial. For a compelling denial of the claim, see Orphanides (2004).
[13] The expression comes from Claudio Borio and Piti Disyatat (2009). Keister, Martin, and McAndrews (2008) instead refer, approvingly, to a floor system as a device for "Divorcing Money from Monetary Policy."
[14] These remarks, once again, refer only to the use of a positive IOER rate to maintain an above-zero interest-rate floor. A *negative* IOER rate can, in contrast, serve in principle to get around the zero lower bound problem by allowing a central bank to maintain a positive opportunity cost of reserve holding even when short-term market rates fall to zero. It is, to say the least, hardly possible that *either* negative or positive (but not zero!) IOER can serve equally well to get around the zero lower bound problem: if one theory of how IOER does this is correct, the other is, presumably, mistaken. I take up this point further in Chapter 9.

When driving an automobile, one can get away with only so many combinations of steering-wheel movements on the one hand and gas pedal pressure on the other. Wouldn't it be nice to be able to have complete freedom to step on the gas and yet steer whichever way we like? Well, there's a solution: put the transmission in neutral! The hitch of course is that while one can now steer any way one likes and stomp on the gas all one likes, one cannot get very far doing either.

A floor system can likewise allow the Fed to steer the fed funds rate any way it likes, while stepping on the reserve-creation pedal as hard as it likes, only by putting the usual monetary transmission mechanism in neutral. For the usual zero lower bound liquidity trap, it substitutes an above-zero liquidity trap in which monetary policy remains, despite appearances to the contrary, more or less equally impotent. The zero lower bound problem is thus avoided, but in a way that might leave the economy no less depressed, and with no more scope for monetary policy stimulus of the old-fashioned sort. It is as if (to offer one last simile), out of concern for would-be jumpers, the designers of a skyscraper decided to construct a broad concrete veranda around their building's second floor to prevent them from ever hitting the ground!

It's true, notwithstanding all that's just been said, that in theory at least, a floor system can achieve any inflation rate or other macroeconomic objective achievable through a corridor system (Ireland 2018). Thus, suppose that there had not been a crisis and recession, that the Fed determined, correctly, that a 150-basis-point policy rate target was consistent with its macroeconomic targets, and that it could—"leaks" aside—achieve that target by establishing a floor system with a 150-basis-point IOER rate while adding to the banking system whatever quantity of additional excess reserves it considered desirable. That arrangement would be equivalent to one in which, without IOER, the Fed simply adjusted the supply of reserves to whatever level was required to keep the effective fed funds rate at 150 basis points. For reasons I'll explain in later chapters, a floor system might ultimately involve higher opportunity costs, depending on how many excess reserves the Fed created,[15] and it might introduce an overtightening bias. But initially at least, the Fed's policy stance would be the same whether the Fed was operating a corridor or floor system.

But now suppose that a crisis caused the macroeconomically optimal IOER rate to plunge to zero, or perhaps even to some negative value. In principle (and setting aside the practical difficulties connected to negative interest rates), Fed authorities could adjust the IOER rate accordingly, and thereby avoid overtightening, while still retaining a floor system. But suppose instead that, out of a desire to avoid the zero lower bound, the authorities decide to set the IOER rate at 25 basis points. By so doing, although they would indeed keep the policy rate at 25 basis points, they would do it at the cost of monetary overtightening. And because they would be overtightening in the context of a floor system, *no ordinary amount of monetary expansion could be counted on to relieve that overtightening,* and even extraordinary expansion couldn't do so by means of the usual monetary transmission mechanism.

The Fed's decision to switch to a floor system at a time when equilibrium market interest rates were collapsing, and to do so with the aim of propping up its policy rate to keep it above a presumed zero lower bound, contributed to the severity of the recession while limiting the Fed's options for promoting recovery. Thanks to it, the U.S. economy remained in the grip of an above-zero liquidity trap years after the nadir of the financial

---

[15] Briefly, while interest on required reserves, paid in strict accordance with the Friedman rule, enhances overall economic welfare, IOER combined with large excess reserve balances reduces it by channeling savings into less productive uses. This last effect isn't allowed for in many formal economic models because they typically fail to allow for differences in the productivity of central and commercial bank assets.

crisis, making the Fed's asset purchases far less effective than they might otherwise have been at reviving overall lending and spending, or at keeping inflation on target. Indeed, as Maria Arias and Yi Wen (2014) explain, because it involved large-scale purchases of long-term debt, and a consequent flattening of the yield curve, Quantitative Easing may actually have reinforced the floor-system-based, above-zero liquidity trap.

★★★

As of early November 2008, though, Fed officials had yet to reckon with how they could possibly stimulate the economy with the Fed's ordinary monetary policy transmission mechanism stuck in neutral, as it were. Until then, stimulating the economy simply wasn't on their minds. Instead, their concern was to *avoid* stimulating the economy unintentionally, and IOER, administered according to the requirements of a floor system, would serve that end well. Alas, in retrospect it seems to have served it all too well.

5

IS THE FLOOR SYSTEM LEGAL?

The Law's Original Intent: A Below-Market IOER Rate

In switching from its circa-2006 plan to use interest payments on reserves for the modest purpose of ending the implicit taxation of bank reserves, to its new plan in which those payments would establish a floor system for monetary control, the Fed had to break, or at least bend, the law. For its new strategy marked a radical change, not just from what the authors of the 2006 legislation had envisioned but from what that legislation allowed for in fact.

The precrisis opinion had been that interest on reserves should be used conservatively and cautiously. Most proposals called for interest to be paid on required reserves only, while all called for rates set low enough to avoid making reserves seem "more attractive relative to alternative short-term assets" (Weiner 1985, p. 30). Otherwise, the prevailing opinion held that interest on reserves, instead of simplifying monetary policy, could further complicate it (ibid).[16]

Such was clearly Federal Reserve Governor Laurence H. Meyer's understanding when, in arguing the case for allowing the

---

[16] See also Laurent and Mote (1985).

Fed to pay interest on reserves before the House Banking Committee in 2000, he explained that

> if the bill becomes law, the Federal Reserve would likely pay an interest rate on required reserve balances close to the rate on other risk-free money market instruments, such as repurchase agreements. This rate is usually a little less than the interest rate on federal funds transactions, which are uncollateralized overnight loans of reserves in the interbank market (Meyer 2000, p. 10).

What Governor Meyer considered an appropriate proxy for "the general level of short-term interest rates" in 2000 was presumably still appropriate in 2006. Because unsecured overnight rates, such as the federal funds rate and the London Interbank Overnight Rate (LIBOR), entail greater risk than overnight repos, to abide by the intent of the 2006 and 2008 laws, the Fed would have to keep the interest rate paid on reserve balances *below* these somewhat riskier overnight interbank lending rates. In this way, as one Fed official explained when the 2006 legislation was being considered, banks would have no reason "to significantly shift their financial resources to take advantage of this [the IOER] rate" (Eubanks 2002, p. 11). Instead, they would continue to keep only such reserve balances as they needed to meet their legal and clearing-balance requirements. The main difference reformers anticipated was that they would no longer bother using sweep accounts to avoid an implicit reserve tax.

The provisions of the 2006 legislation reflected these same considerations. According to section 201 of Title II of that measure, the Fed may pay interest on depository institutions' reserve balances "at a rate or rates not to exceed the general level of short-term interest rates."

Above the Law?

Except for a change in dates, the Emergency Economic Stabilization Act of 2008 left the details of the 2006 Act unaltered.

Fed officials therefore found themselves in a quandary. As we've seen, they wanted to be able to resort to IOER three years ahead of schedule precisely for the purpose of making excess reserves "*attractive* relative to alternative short-term assets" (emphasis added). That meant setting the IOER rate *above* the going, still positive (but below target) equilibrium fed funds rate. Indeed, given the "leakiness" of the Fed's floor system, the IOER rate would have to be set *considerably* above the Fed's target rate. That necessarily meant keeping the IOER rate above other, comparable market-based short-term interest rates. Yet by law, as we've seen, the Fed was only supposed to pay interest on bank reserve balances at a rate "not to exceed the general level of short-term interest rates."

That the Fed's IOER rates were well above comparable market rates can be seen in Figures 5.1 and 5.2. Figure 5.1 compares the IOER rate to both the effective federal funds and the LIBOR rate.

Figure 5.1: IOER, Overnight LIBOR, and Effective Federal Funds Rates

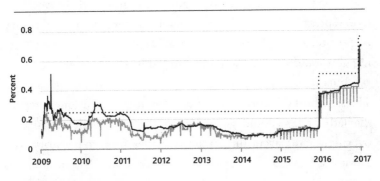

···· Interest Rate on Excess Reserves
—— Overnight London Interbank Offered Rate (LIBOR), based on U.S. Dollar
—— Effective Federal Funds Rate

Sources: Federal Reserve Bank of St. Louis FRED Database; ICE Benchmark Administration; Federal Reserve Bank of New York.

Figure 5.2: IOER and GCF Treasury Repo Rates

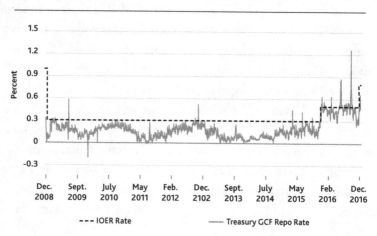

Because the fed funds and LIBOR rates are rates for unsecured overnight loans, they include a small risk component, while the IOER rate is equivalent to a risk-free overnight rate. For that reason, and as Governor Meyer suggested in his previously mentioned testimony, the rate implicit in overnight, Treasury-secured repurchase agreements might be a more appropriate market-rate benchmark. As Figure 5.2 shows, that overnight rate, represented by the GCF (general collateral finance) Treasury Repo rate, an index produced by the Depository Trust and Clearing Corporation, has also tended to fall below the IOER rate.

Finally, it's instructive to compare the IOER rate to rates on Treasury bills of various maturities. Owing to their longer terms, the latter rates should generally be above equivalent, risk-free overnight rates, according to the securities' term to maturity. Yet, as Figure 5.3 shows, rates on both 4-week and 3-month T-bills have also been persistently, often substantially, below the IOER rate. Indeed, from the spring of 2011 through midsummer of 2015, even rates on 1-year Treasury bills remained below, generally well below, the IOER rate.

Figure 5.3: IOER and Treasury Bill Rates

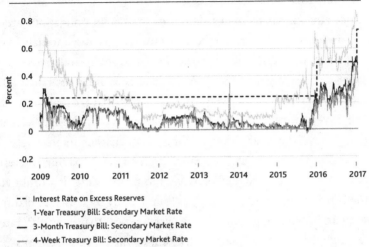

-- Interest Rate on Excess Reserves
--- 1-Year Treasury Bill: Secondary Market Rate
— 3-Month Treasury Bill: Secondary Market Rate
— 4-Week Treasury Bill: Secondary Market Rate

Source: Federal Reserve Bank of St. Louis FRED Database.

In short, it's impossible to reconcile the Federal Reserve's setting of its IOER rate with any *reasonable* understanding of the law's stipulation that it is "not to exceed the general level of short-term interest rates."

"One of these rates is not like the others . . ."

In an apparent after-the-fact attempt to legalize the Fed's IOER rate settings, Fed officials, in drafting the final rules implementing the 2008 statute, as announced in the *Federal Register* on June 22, 2015, determined that for the purpose of setting IOER

> "short-term interest rates" are rates on obligations with maturities of no more than one year, such as the primary credit rate and rates on term federal funds, term repurchase agreements, commercial paper, term Eurodollar deposits, and other similar instruments (Regulation D: Reserve Requirements for Depository Institutions 2015, p. 35567).

While most of the listed rates are unobjectionable, even if they fail to include overnight obligations (which are, after all, closer equivalents to reserve balances than term obligations are), the presence of the primary credit rate is a glaring anomaly, for that's the discount rate that the Fed charges sound banks for short-term emergency loans. As such, it isn't a market rate at all but one set administratively by the Fed's Board of Governors. Moreover, since 2003 the Fed has always set its primary credit rate "above the usual level of short-term market interest rates" (Board of Governors 2017b). Since the Fed began paying interest on reserves, it has also deliberately set its primary credit rate above the IOER rate.[17] The Fed has thus found a way by which to claim, with an implicit appeal to Chevron deference, that its IOER rate settings have after all been consistent with the requirements of the 2006 law![18]

That the Fed should thumb its nose at the statute granting it the authority to pay interest on reserves would be regrettable enough if its doing so had only benign consequences. But that's far from being the case. On the contrary, by bending the law to conform to its plan to make the accumulation of reserve balances more attractive to banks than other forms of investment, the Fed fundamentally altered the workings of the U.S. monetary system, with regrettable consequences for the U.S. economy.

---

[17] Since the beginning of 2010, the Fed has maintained a fixed spread of 50 basis points between the IOER rate and the primary credit rate by adjusting both rates together.

[18] "Chevron deference" is the controversial principle, put into effect by the Supreme Court's 1984 decision in *Chevron USA v. Natural Resources Defense Council, Inc.*, that courts should defer to government agencies' own interpretations of statutes establishing new agency obligations and powers. In *City of Arlington v. FCC* (2013), the Court held, furthermore, that government agencies deserve deference even when it comes to interpreting statutes establishing the scope of their own authority!

6

THE FLOOR SYSTEM AND INTERBANK LENDING

Goodbye Fed Funds Market

As we've seen, when the Fed began paying interest on bank reserves, its immediate concern was to keep its emergency lending from causing the fed funds rate to drop below 1.5 percent—the target it set when it announced its IOER plan. To repeat Ben Bernanke's words, "by setting the interest rate we paid on reserves high enough, we could prevent the federal funds rate from falling too low, no matter how much [emergency] lending we did" (Bernanke 2015).

But interest on reserves could not discourage banks from placing *newly created* reserves into the fed funds market without discouraging them from supplying *any* funds to that market: if a dollar of reserves that landed in a bank's Fed account as a result of the Fed's post-Lehman emergency lending earned more sitting in that account than it could earn if lent to another bank overnight, the same was true of a dollar of reserves held beforehand.[19] Consequently, as Figure 6.1 shows, IOER served not only to keep fresh reserves from lowering the fed funds rate, but to dramatically reduce the total volume

---

[19] Increasing the quantity of reserves itself would normally have *increased* the volume of interbank lending as long as the Fed saw to it "that there is an opportunity cost to holding reserves, by remunerating them at a rate below the market rate" (Borio and Disyatat 2009, p. 18, n29).

Figure 6.1: Fed Funds Lending, 2006–2012

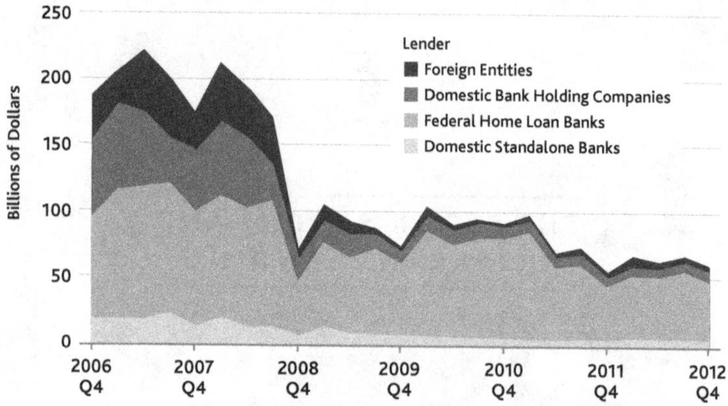

Source: Quarterly call report data.

of lending on the fed funds market. Whereas financial institutions lent over $200 billion daily on the fed funds market during the last quarter of 2007, by the end of 2012 that figure had fallen to just $60 billion (Afonso, Entz, and LeSueur 2013). Although the figure has since returned to the neighborhood of $90-$100 billion, allowing for concurrent growth in overall nominal spending, the fed funds market remains relatively quiescent.

This outcome was, after all, fully predictable. Indeed, William Whitesell (2006, p. 1183), who was then Deputy Associate Director of the Board of Governors' Division of Monetary Affairs, predicted it not long before the crisis. Commenting on the potential advantages of a floor system relative to a symmetric corridor system, he observed that, with its interest rate on reserves equal to the target interest rate, the floor system would have the advantage of insulating interest rates from the central bank's reserve supply errors. However, he also recognized a downside, namely that "trading in the overnight market might dry up," with potentially "deleterious effects on market functioning."

Once the Fed's floor system was in place, and as the Fed continued to expand the stock of reserve balances, banks and bank holding companies (BHCs) that were eligible for IOER became less and less inclined to rely on overnight funding, until most ceased to rely on it at all. Only the Federal Home Loan Banks and (for a time) some other GSEs continued to lend as much as ever, for the sake of securing a share of banks' IOER earnings. The fed funds market thus ceased to function, as it had for decades, as banks' preferred and most reliable source of last-minute liquidity, having instead been transformed to a substantial degree into a mere vehicle for bank-to-GSE interest-rate arbitrage.

Because banks that were once regular participants in the fed funds market no longer had reason to manage their liquidity by means of overnight lending and borrowing, they also lacked an important former reason to scrutinize one another and to thereby contain systemic risk, to wit: a desire to avoid incurring losses on unsecured loans. Economists Jean-Charles Rochet and Jean Tirole (1996, p. 735) were among the first to draw attention to the advantages of interbank peer monitoring, while warning that, insofar as it discourages such monitoring, "government intervention . . . destroys the very benefit of a decentralized [banking] system":

> If one does not believe that the fine information that banks have or may acquire about each other can be used fruitfully, or else [one believes] that similar information can be acquired and utilized efficiently by regulatory authorities, then there is no particular reason to encourage decentralized interactions among banks. Alternatively, one may argue that this reformist view of cutting interbank linkages amounts to throwing the baby out with the bathwater, and that one should preserve the current flexibility while improving banks' incentive to cross-monitor.[20]

---

[20] Marie Hoerva and Cyrol Monnet (2016, p. 2) also find that money markets, and unsecured interbank markets especially, "can provide market discipline, which we define as an ex ante provision of incentives to banks to conduct business in a safe and sound manner. The bilateral interaction between a borrower and its lender in the money market ensures that incentives to take on excessive risk are tamed."

In a later study drawing on Rochet and Tirole's work, Craig Furfine (2001, p. 34) finds that when banks were inclined to "lend significant amounts of money to one another every day in the federal funds market," as they did until the advent of interest on reserves, they had "an incentive to monitor their counterparties and to price these loans as a function of . . . the credit risk of the borrowing bank." Furthermore, the rates charged in actual fed funds transactions really did reflect the varying credit risk of different institutions, with "banks with higher profitability, higher capital ratios, and fewer problem loans pay[ing] lower rates" than others (ibid.). Banks were able, in other words, to "distinguish credit risk among their peers and price loan contracts accordingly" (ibid., p. 54). Risk premiums were, however, visible only for those banks that weren't considered all that likely to default. In contrast, those having "a significant perceived possibility of default" found themselves altogether excluded from the federal funds market, from which they might borrow only at such high rates as would make their distress all the more notorious.

Studies undertaken since the crisis confirm Furfine's earlier findings. They also offer further grounds for supposing that, by shutting down interbank lending on the fed funds market, the Fed's switch to a floor system destroyed an important promoter of interbank monitoring—and an important source of information about individual banks' health. A study by Christophe Pérignon, David Thesmar, and Guillaume Villemey (2018) looks at the euro-denominated CD (certificates of deposit) market, which accounted for a large share of Eurozone wholesale lending between 2008 and 2014. Like overnight federal funds loans, CDs are short-term debt securities that resemble overnight fed funds loans in being unsecured. Consequently, their purchasers—mainly money-market funds—have reason to care about the health of banks that issue them. The authors find that funding "dry-ups," meaning occasions when banks largely or entirely ceased to sell CDs, were generally both bank specific and driven by information about banks' health, including their profitability, capitalization, and the quality of their assets. Funding dry-ups also proved to be a good predictor of a bank's *future* poor health. In short, despite extreme market stress, sophisticated lenders were able to inform themselves of banks' creditworthiness and, by signaling that creditworthiness by driving less worthy banks out of the CD market, to supply useful information to other lenders.

In a complementary study, the European Central Bank's Esa Jokivuolle, Eero Tölö, and Matti Virén (2015) look at average overnight lending rates charged to individual participants in the Eurosystem's TARGET2 large value payment system and compare them to an overnight rate index. They find that the difference supplied "additional early-warning indications on certain banks' deteriorating financial health over and above bank CDS [Credit Default Swap] spreads," and that it could therefore "provide useful information of [sic] the health of banks which do not have a traded CDS contract."[21]

Finally, a recent study by several Dutch economists (Blasques, Bräuning, and Lelyveld 2016) finds that bank-to-bank monitoring contributed to a significant decline in interbank credit risk uncertainty, and a corresponding increase in the volume of interbank lending, on the Dutch interbank market. Its authors also report what they refer to as a "multiplier effect" of banks' peer monitoring efforts, whereby lenders were inspired to redouble their monitoring efforts as the perceived

---

[21] A Credit Default Swap (CDS) resembles a marketable insurance policy sold by larger banks to investors in their credit instruments to protect those investors against losses in the event the bank defaults. Because the value of the CDS depends on the perceived health of the bank that issues it, the market price of a bank's CDSs can be taken as a signal of the bank's health.

risks of interbank lending declined, because the decline in risk made it worthwhile for them to widen the set of counterparties with which they might choose to interact. Lastly, the authors explain that a relatively wide interest-rate corridor is crucial to the encouragement of interbank monitoring. To secure "the benefits obtainable from peer monitoring," they conclude, a central bank must

> consider policies that increase the rate differential between the interbank market and [its] standing facilities for depositing and lending funds. Only then is the interbank market profitable enough to encourage intense peer monitoring and search among banks (ibid., p. 39).

IOER versus Perceived Counterparty Risk

The fact that very risky borrowers are likely to be altogether excluded from unsecured interbank markets may appear to lend credibility to the claim that the post–Lehman collapse in fed funds lending was due not to interest on excess reserves but to a persistent post–Lehman increase in perceived counterparty risk. But perceived counterparty risk is no more capable of explaining the *persistent* decline in interbank lending than it is of explaining banks' persistent accumulation of excess reserves, which I discuss at length in the next chapter. Although the TED spread—a popular measure of the perceived counterparty risk, equal to the difference between the interest rate on short-term interbank lending and the interest rate on Treasury securities—spiked at the time of Lehman's failure, it began to decline soon afterwards when the Fed decided to come to AIG's rescue, eventually falling to levels even lower than those that prevailed before the crisis. Interbank lending, on the other hand, never recovered. The Fed's decision to pay interest on excess reserves, and the ensuing growth in banks' excess reserve balances, therefore appear to have been the fundamental cause of the enduring post-Lehman decline in interbank lending.[22]

The close relationship between the total volume of interbank lending and the opportunity cost of reserve holding, as measured by the difference between the interbank lending rates and the IOER rate, also supports the view that the Fed's adoption of a floor system was to blame for the subsequent decline in interbank lending. Although the relationship is similar for all banks, it is clearest for foreign banks, which (given their prominent role in IOER-rate arbitrage) have been especially inclined to accumulate excess reserves. As Figure 6.2 shows, the precipitous decline in the opportunity cost of reserves, brought about by the Fed's decision to pay interest on excess reserves, coincided with

Figure 6.2: Interbank Lending and the LIBOR-IOER Spread

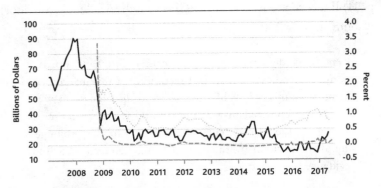

— Interbank Loans, Foreign-Related Institutions (left)

······ 12-Month London Interbank Offered Rate (LIBOR), based on U.S. Dollar-Interest Rate on Excess Reserves (right)

— — 1-Month London Interbank Offered Rate (LIBOR), based on U.S. Dollar-Interest Rate on Excess Reserves (right)

Sources: Federal Reserve Bank of St. Louis FRED Database; ICE Benchmark Administration.

---

[22] Bech et al. (2015) offer interesting insights concerning the combined effects on wholesale lending of the fears raised by Lehman's failure and the Fed's IOER announcement.

an equally precipitous initial decline in foreign-bank interbank loans.

Finally, it was not only in the United States that the switch from a corridor-style to a floor-style operating system coincided with a marked decline in interbank lending. The same thing happened elsewhere where floor systems were resorted to, including Norway (Sellin and Åsberg 2014), the UK (Winters 2012, p. 40), New Zealand (Selgin 2018), and the Eurozone (Garcia-de-Andoain et al. 2016 and van den End 2017). According to Bill Winters (2012, p. 40; see also Jackson and Sim 2013, pp. 225–26), after its own switch to a floor system in March 2009, the Bank of England found that it had become other UK banks' "preferred counterparty" for short-term lending, "disintermediating the interbank money market and thereby inhibiting interbank money market activity." Jan Willem van Den End (2017, p. 11) likewise reports that the ECB's switch to a "de facto" floor system[23] in July 2009

> went in tandem with falling unsecured interbank transactions . . . , indicating that the functioning of this market segment was impaired. While it is hard to disentangle to what extent the impaired market functioning relates to the crisis (to which the Eurosystem responded) or to the prolonged liquidity provision by the central bank, literature also finds evidence for the latter.

---

[23] Because the EONIA (Euro Over-Night Index Average) rate targeted by the ECB has typically been several basis points higher than the ECB's deposit rate, the ECB's system superficially resembles an asymmetrical corridor rather than a floor system. According to Francesco Papadia (2014), a former Director General for Market Operations at the ECB, the persistence of this spread since 2009 has been due to the fact that the EONIA rate is biased upward by special overnight borrowing arrangements between two sets of publicly owned German banks—the Sparkassen (regional public savings banks) and the larger Landesbanken, which mainly engage in wholesale lending and are owned mainly by associations of regional savings banks and their respective federal states.

European banks' "diminished appetite for [interbank] lending" in turn

> created an even larger dependence on central bank funding by banks with a liquidity shortage. So bank behavior act[ed] as a feedback mechanism, reinforcing the transition to a floor system. That the floor system has persisted for nearly eight years now indicates . . . a critical transition to a new equilibrium [in which] central bank liquidity supply has crowded out private intermediation (ibid., pp. 12–13).

From Lender of Last Resort to Borrower of First Resort

In the United States, as in the Eurozone, the collapse of interbank lending created a further motive, beyond the return on reserves itself, for banks to accumulate excess reserves. That's because, with the collapse in the volume of federal funds lending, banks that once routinely relied on overnight unsecured loans to meet their liquidity needs discovered that doing so was no longer prudent. Because that collapse at first caught many banks by surprise, its immediate effect was a sharp spike, on October 7, 2008, in the fed funds rate, which rose to 2.97 percent, or almost twice the Fed's target at the time. Consequently, even those banks that might not have found the IOER rate itself all that tempting responded to the new regime by equipping themselves with precautionary reserve cushions to cover unanticipated reserve outflows they would previously have covered using borrowed funds.

As Gara Afonso, Anna Kovner, and Antoinette Schoar (2011, p. 1109) point out, until these changes came about, the fed funds market had long served as "the most immediate source of liquidity for regulated banks in the U.S." Consequently, any disruption of that market could "lead to inadequate allocation of capital and lack of risk sharing between banks." In extreme cases, they add, it might "even trigger bank runs."

In few words, by establishing a floor system, the Fed, which is supposed to serve as a lender of last resort, became a short-term *borrower* of *first* resort, destroying in the process the inter-bank lending market that had long served as banks' traditional, first-resort source of last-minute liquidity.

7

THE FLOOR SYSTEM AND
RESERVE HOARDING

Apart from its effect on interbank lending, the most notorious consequence of the Fed's interest payments on excess reserves has been unprecedented growth in banks' excess reserves balances, meaning Fed balances held by banks beyond the requirement to meet their minimum legal reserve requirements, together with banks' holdings of vault cash.

As of June 2018, the IOER rate is 195 basis points. But from December 2008 until December 2015, the rate was a mere 25 basis points. Many observers doubt that that low rate could not have sufficed to substantially alter banks' portfolio allocations by causing banks to accumulate excess reserves or otherwise. Paul Krugman (2014) even accuses those claiming that interest on reserves encouraged banks to hoard reserves of failing a "reality test." "Of course, it wasn't interest on reserves," he writes, "as both the 30s case and Japan show."

But, at best, all that the U.S. experience of the 1930s and Japan's more recent experience show is that interest on reserves isn't a *necessary* cause of reserve hoarding.[24] They hardly suffice to show that it can't be a *sufficient* cause. Moreover, if believing that

---

[24] Concerning whether the U.S. economy was really in a zero-lower-bound liquidity trap in the 1930s, see above, note 11. I discuss Japan's experience in Chapter 13.

a seemingly modest IOER rate could sponsor reserve hoarding meant failing a reality test, then Fed officials themselves, including Ben Bernanke, must also have failed that test. As we've seen, they sought permission to pay interest on bank reserves for the express purpose of getting banks to hoard them.

More importantly, those modest IOER rates weren't modest *relative to comparable market rates.* For that reason, their influence on banks' behavior has been anything but trivial. As Simon Potter (2015), a Federal Reserve Bank of New York Vice President (and head of its Market Group) explains,

> The IOER rate is essentially the rate of return earned by a bank on a riskless overnight deposit held at the Fed, thus representing the opportunity cost to a bank of using its funds in an alternative manner, such as making a loan or purchasing a security. In principle, *no bank would want to deploy its funds in a way that earned less than what can be earned from its balances maintained at the Fed* (emphasis added).

Thanks to IOER, U.S. banks and foreign bank branches did in fact refrain from acquiring any assets bearing a net return below what they might earn simply by retaining Fed reserve balances. Some, indeed, found it worthwhile to actively acquire Fed balances for the sake of arbitraging the spread between the return on such balances and private-market borrowing costs.

The Accumulation and Distribution of Excess Reserves

In the two decades prior to October 2008, banks generally held between \$1 and \$2 billion in excess reserves, in part for the sake of avoiding shortfalls from their required reserves, but mainly to avoid relatively costly clearing overdrafts. (The few exceptions consisted of short-lived spikes in excess reserves following crises like that of September 11, 2001, when banks briefly held over \$19 billion in excess reserves.) Banks' minimum reserve

Figure 7.1: Balances

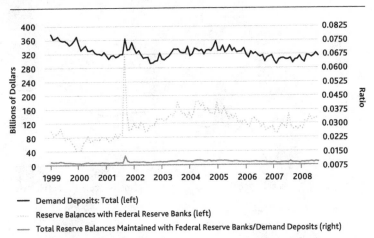

Source: Federal Reserve Bank of St. Louis FRED Database.

requirements were, in contrast, largely met by their holdings of vault cash. Between them, minimum reserve requirements and banks' demand for excess reserves for settlement purposes determined banks' overall need for reserve balances, together with their desired ratio of such balances to their demand deposits. As Figure 7.1 shows, reserve balances normally amounted to between one-fifth and two-fifths of 1 percent of demand deposits only.

As the next figure (7.2) shows, following Lehman Brothers' failure, banks' excess reserve holdings began growing in lock-step with growth in the monetary base (the sum of total bank reserves and currency held by the public), starting with growth in the base fueled by the Fed's post-Lehman emergency lending and continuing, after March 2009, with several rounds of large-scale asset purchases (LSAPs) or "Quantitative Easing." By August 2014 excess reserves, which had rarely surpassed $2 billion before the crisis, had risen to almost $2.7 *trillion*.

The sharp increase in perceived counterparty risk that immediately followed Lehman's failure itself accounted, to be sure, for

Figure 7.2: Excess Reserves and the Monetary Base

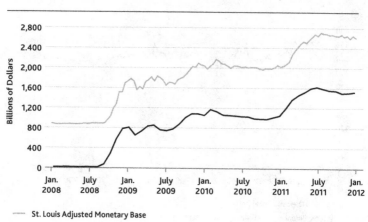

--- St. Louis Adjusted Monetary Base
— Excess Reserves of Depository Institutions

Source: Federal Reserve Bank of St. Louis FRED Database.

some increase in banks' desire for excess reserves at that time. But as I noted in the previous chapter, in discussing the collapse of interbank lending, the increase in perceived risk, as measured by the TED spread, was only temporary; as Figure 7.3 suggests, that temporary increase can't account for banks' willingness to continue accumulating excess reserves long after the panic had subsided.

That an above-market IOER rate alone could cause banks to cling to any new reserves that came their way should not have surprised anyone.[25] As Finadium's Jonathan Cooper (2012)

---

[25] For theories, see Dutkowsky and VanHoose (2017) and Ireland (2018). According to the latter's DSGE ("dynamic stochastic general equilibrium") model, in the absence of positive costs of managing large excess reserve holdings, banks receiving interest on reserves at an above-market rate will wish to hold "an unboundedly large stock of reserves." To avoid that outcome, the IOER rate must be set slightly *below* the market rate (ibid., pp. 28–29). Bewley (1980) and Sargent and Wallace (1985) were among the first authors to draw attention to the problem of reserve demand indeterminacy in an IOER regime with a return on bank reserves at least equal to that on nonreserve assets.

Figure 7.3: TED Spread and Excess Reserves

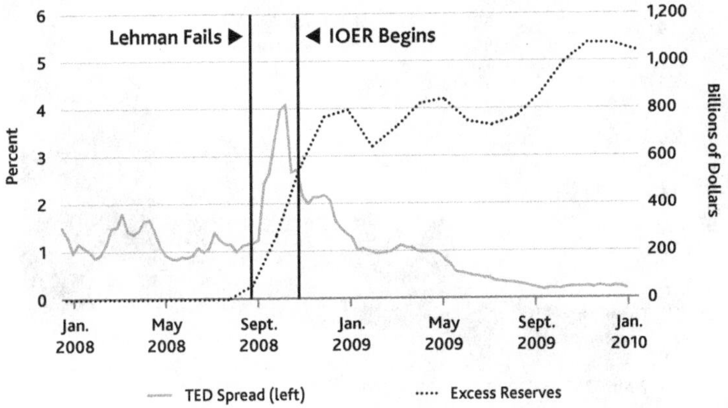

Source: Federal Reserve Bank of St. Louis FRED Database.

observed in August 2012, although the Fed was only paying 25 basis points on reserves, that was enough to keep "lots of cash out of the securities market" since "[y]ou have to go out to 2 year notes before [U.S. Treasury security] rates match the 25 [basis points] that the Fed is paying."

Still, banks didn't all take part equally in the vast reserve buildup. Instead, as Figures 7.4 and 7.5 show, most of the new reserves ended up at the very largest U.S. banks or at U.S. branches of foreign banks. As of early 2015, the top 25 U.S. banks, by asset size, held more than half of all outstanding bank reserves, with the top three alone holding 21 percent of the total, while foreign bank branches accounted for most of the rest. The cash assets of small U.S. banks, in contrast, rose only modestly.

That the very largest banks secured a disproportionate share of the total accumulation of excess reserves is partly explained by the fact that those banks included some of the primary dealers that served as the Fed's immediate counterparties in its asset purchases (Craig, Millington, and Zito 2014). Having thus had "first dibs" on new reserves the Fed created, primary dealer banks simply

Figure 7.4: Excess Reserves, by Bank Asset Size, 2006–2015

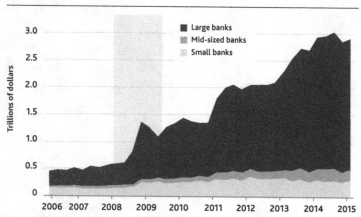

Note: Shaded bar indicates the recession.
Source: Quarterly call report data.

Figure 7.5: Excess Reserves, Foreign and Domestic Banks, 2006–2015

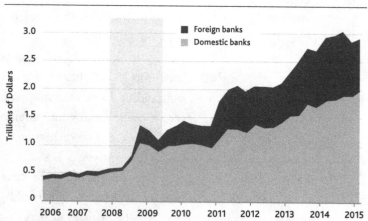

Note: Shaded bar indicates the recession.
Source: Quarterly call report data.

refrained from letting go of reserves they acquired. That practice was, of course, quite contrary to what primary dealers were normally expected to do, and to what they generally did do before the crisis, when the Fed was still relying on its traditional means of monetary control. Indeed, in the early stages of the subprime crisis, Fed officials worried that the collapse of ailing primary dealers would prevent them from serving as reliable conduits through which fresh reserves would make their way from the Fed to the rest of the banking system (e.g., Kohn 2009). Now, paradoxically, IOER was itself serving to close the same conduits, along with much of the rest of the interbank market, and was doing so deliberately as part of the Fed's new monetary control strategy.

As for the disproportionate quantity of excess reserves accumulated by U.S. branches of foreign-owned banks, it is partly accounted for by the fact that many of them hold no retail deposits and therefore aren't subject to FDIC insurance premium assessments. U.S. banks, on the other hand, *are* generally subject to those assessments. Starting in April 2011, FDIC premiums, which were previously assessed against banks' U.S. deposits, have instead been assessed against their total assets, including their excess reserve balances, less tangible equity. For that reason, and because many of their (mostly European) parent companies enjoy much lower net interest margins than U.S. banks, foreign bank branches have found it especially profitable to acquire fed funds for the sake of arbitraging the difference between the Fed's IOER rate and lower private-market interest rates. Foreign banks have consequently ended up playing a particularly important part in keeping growth in the total quantity of reserve balances from contributing to corresponding growth in overall bank lending.[26]

---

[26] According to Ayelen Banegas and Manjola Tase (2017, p. 14), as a result of the April 2011 change in FDIC fee assessments, U.S. banks' net return on reserve balances initially declined by about 10 basis points. Since then, however, reduced FDIC assessments, reflecting banks' improved conditions, have reversed the greater part of that decline.

That very large U.S. banks and foreign bank branches have been especially inclined to hoard Fed reserve balances does not mean that small banks refrained altogether from doing so. As we've seen, by cutting off the flow of interbank funds, the Fed's above-market IOER rate made it necessary for banks that still found excess reserves less remunerative than other assets to accumulate such reserves to protect themselves against the risk of occasional large reserve outflows, such as go hand-in-hand with lending. As the late Ronald McKinnon (2011) observed in a *Wall Street Journal* op-ed,

> Banks with good retail lending opportunities typically lend by opening credit lines to nonbank customers. But these credit lines are open-ended in the sense that the commercial borrower can choose when—and by how much—he will actually draw on his credit line. This creates uncertainty for the bank in not knowing what its future cash positions will be. An illiquid bank could be in trouble if its customers simultaneously decided to draw down their credit lines.

Ordinarily, McKinnon continued, banks can cover their unexpected reserve shortfalls by borrowing funds from other banks on the interbank market. But banks with surplus reserves may "become loath to part with them for a derisory yield," while those that find themselves short "cannot easily bid for funds at an interest rate significantly above the prevailing interbank rate without inadvertently signaling that they might be in trouble." Interbank borrowing therefore ceases to be an attractive alternative to maintaining higher excess reserve cushions, even where the marginal return on reserves is less than that on loans. In fact, since late 2008 the "prevailing interbank rate" was irrelevant: To get other banks to lend to them on the federal funds market, banks would have had to offer more than the going IOER rate, which was itself higher than short-term market rates. Needless to say, virtually none of them ever did.

The Quicksand Effect

Although the Fed's modest interest payments on excess reserves succeeded in getting banks to accumulate vast quantities of such reserves, it doesn't follow that restoring the IOER rate to zero would inspire banks to rid themselves of most of the excess reserves they've accumulated. The reason has to do with the immense growth in the total supply of reserve balances that has since taken place, for under a floor system *the greater the nominal stock of bank reserves, the more the IOER rate must be lowered to reduce the quantity of excess reserves demanded to zero.* In other words, the more liquidity the central bank supplies to an economy in an IOER-based liquidity trap, the deeper it becomes mired in that trap. Call it "the quicksand effect."

The quicksand effect is easily illustrated by looking again at a diagram illustrating the demand for and supply of federal funds under a floor system. In Figure 7.6, the supply schedule for bank reserves (or federal funds) is, as usual, shown as a vertical line, which shifts to the right as the Fed acquires assets, and to the left as it disposes of them. The reserve demand schedule, on the other hand, slopes downward, but only until it reaches the going IOER rate, here initially assumed to be set at 25 basis points. At that point the demand schedule becomes horizontal,

Figure 7.6: The Quicksand Effect

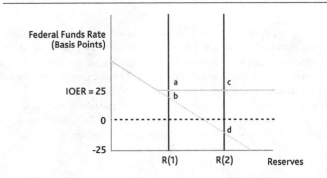

because banks would rather accumulate excess reserves that yield
the IOER rate than lend reserves overnight for an even lower
return.[27]

For the initial stock of reserves R(1), starting at the equilibrium point "a," a slight reduction in the IOER rate would
suffice to get the banking system back onto the sloped part of
its reserve demand schedule, at point "b," where reserves are
again scarce at the margin. But once the stock of reserves has
increased to R(2), it takes a much more substantial reduction in
the IOER rate—perhaps, as the move in the illustration from
"c" to "d" suggests, even into negative territory—to make
reserves scarce at the margin again. No less dramatic reduction
in the IOER rate would suffice to provoke a switch back to a
corridor system without any accompanying central bank asset
sales.[28]

Because the move from "c" to "d," like that from "a" to "b,"
involves no change in the total stock of bank reserves, readers
may be tempted to assume that it also involves no reduction in the
quantity of *excess* reserves, and hence no change in banks' inclination to hoard such reserves. The temptation should be resisted:
although banks hold the same total quantity of reserves at "d"
as at "c," the first of these equilibrium states involves a higher
quantity of bank lending and deposit creation, hence a higher
value of required reserves, with a correspondingly lower value of
excess reserves.

---

[27] For the sake of simplicity, the diagram assumes an unchanging, downward-sloping reserve demand schedule, with both actual and "shadow" (below
IOER) components. In practice any policy changes that serve to increase bank
lending, spending, and the rate of inflation will tend to shift that schedule
rightwards, altering equilibrium values accordingly.
[28] Just how much difference it would have made had the IOER rate been
reduced to zero once quantitative easing—meaning the Fed's three rounds of
large-scale asset purchases—was well underway, is a question we'll ponder in
Chapter 9.

Excess Reserves and the Fed's Balance Sheet

Some economists nevertheless insist that, instead of depending on the interest rate paid on bank reserves, the post-Lehman accumulation of excess bank reserves was an inevitable consequence of the Fed's asset purchases. In an influential *Liberty Street* post, for example, Gaetona Antinolfi and Todd Keister (2012) criticized Alan Blinder (2012) and others for claiming that lowering the IOER rate would have any influence at all upon banks' demand for excess reserves:

> Because lowering the interest rate paid on reserves wouldn't change the quantity of assets held by the Fed, it must not change the total size of the monetary base either. Moreover, lowering this interest rate to zero (or even slightly below zero) is unlikely to induce banks, firms, or households to start holding large quantities of currency. It follows, therefore, that lowering the interest rate paid on excess reserves will not have any meaningful effect on the quantity of balances banks hold on deposit at the Fed. . . . In fact, the total quantity of reserve balances held by banks conveys no information about their lending activities—it simply reflects the Federal Reserve's decisions on how many assets to acquire (Keister and Antinolfi 2012).

It's of course true, as any money and banking textbook will affirm, that banks cannot alter the total quantity of reserve balances simply by trading them for other assets, as doing so only transfers the balances to other banks. But the question isn't whether a lower IOER rate would reduce *total* reserves. It's whether it would result in a lower quantity of *excess* reserves. The answer to that question is "yes," because, as the same textbooks also explain, as banks trade unwanted reserves for other assets, they also contribute to the growth of total banking system deposits; the fact that unwanted reserves get passed on like so many hot potatoes only makes deposits grow that much more rapidly. The growth of total deposits serves in turn to convert former excess reserves into required reserves, where "required" means required either to meet minimum legal requirements or for banks' clearing needs.

That, at least, is what always happened before the Fed began encouraging banks to cling to excess reserves. For example, as Figure 7.7 shows, until October 2008 banks routinely disposed of unwanted excess reserves in the manner just described, thereby keeping system excess reserves at trivial levels, and doing so despite additions to the total supply of bank reserves that were, by pre-2008 standards at least, far from trivial. For example, as Donald Dutkowsky and David VanHoose (2017, p. 1) point out, "from January 1997 to September 2008 the monetary base nearly doubled, from $463 billion to $910 billion. Yet the share of bank assets held as excess reserves remained near zero throughout."

It follows that when banks hold a large quantity of *excess* reserves, that fact actually conveys very significant "information about their lending activities." Specifically, it tells us that something has caused them to refrain from engaging in such activities precisely to the extent that they choose to accumulate reserves instead.

Figure 7.7: Total and Excess Reserve Balances, 1984–2008

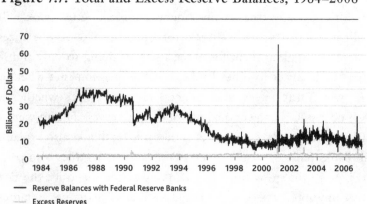

Source: Federal Reserve Bank of St. Louis FRED Database.

In reply to these observations, Professor Keister has suggested[29] that, floor system or no floor system, the unprecedented scale of the Fed's post-Lehman balance sheet growth would have rendered the traditional means by which banks disposed of unwanted excess reserves inoperable. Banks, he says, couldn't possibly achieve the expansion in their total assets and deposit liabilities required to convert so vast an increase in total reserves into an equally vast increase in required reserves.

But Keister's counter-argument is also contradicted by relevant historical evidence, consisting of instances of hyperinflation in which central banks expanded their balance sheets on a scale much larger still than that seen in the United States since 2008. During the notorious Weimar hyperinflation, for example, the (proportional) growth in German bank reserves far exceeded that witnessed in the United States since Lehman's bankruptcy. Yet according to Frank D. Graham (1930, p. 68), Germany's banks, far from accumulating excess reserves, increased their lending more than proportionately. "It would appear," Graham writes, "that the commercial banks extended loans throughout the period of post-war inflation considerably in excess of a proportionate relationship with the increase in the monetary base. . . . The increase in deposits issuing from loans was especially marked in 1922 and till stabilization in 1923."

It doesn't follow, of course, that in the absence of interest on excess reserves, the Fed's post-Lehman asset purchases would have led to hyperinflation. Had banks not been inclined to hoard reserves, Fed officials would not have dared to purchase assets on such a large scale: had they tried doing so, they would have been compelled to end the purchases as soon as it became evident that the rate of inflation was in danger of exceeding the Fed's target. As it was, by relying on IOER to discourage banks from

---

[29] In personal correspondence.

FLOORED!

dispensing with excess reserves, the Fed ended up falling short of, instead of surpassing, its inflation target. That outcome came as a surprise to those accustomed to the workings of the Fed's traditional monetary control framework. But in the context of its new floor framework, any tendency for the Fed's asset purchases to raise prices would itself have been surprising.

Excess Reserves and the Liquidity Coverage Ratio

Others may wonder whether, rather than being due to excess reserves' high yield relative to other assets, banks' continuing willingness to hold substantial quantities of such reserves has been a result of their need to satisfy Basel's Liquidity Coverage Ratio (LCR) requirements. The Basel requirements, which were first applied to U.S. banks at the beginning of 2015, call for bank holding companies having at least $250 billion in assets, or ones with $10 billion or more in foreign exposure, to maintain a level of "High Quality Liquid Assets" (HQLAs) against their "nonoperating" deposits equal to 100 percent of their 30-day liquidity outflows.[30]

Although banks' required reserves do not count as HQLAs for the purpose of satisfying LCR requirements, their excess reserves do. Consequently, it's possible that with the Basel LCR requirements now in effect, even if reducing the IOER rate would have made a difference in the past, it would no longer lead to any substantial reduction in banks' demand for excess reserves. Credit Swiss's Zoltan Pozsar (2016, pp. 2–3), for one, appears to take this view. "Contrary to conventional wisdom," he says, "there are no excess reserves—not one penny":

---

[30] Operating deposits include retail deposits and wholesale deposits held for clearing, custody, or cash management purchases. All other unsecured wholesale deposits are considered nonoperating.

Labelling the trillions of reserves created as a byproduct of QE as "excess" was appropriate only until the Liquidity Coverage Ratio (LCR) went live, but not after. . . . Before the LCR, excess reserves were indeed excess: every penny was in excess of the amount of reserves required by the Federal Reserve's Regulation D. Under the LCR, all excess reserves became required: not to comply with Regulation D, but with the LCR. . . . It is helpful to think about the LCR as a *global* reserve requirement regime. . . . Excess reserves are not sloshing but rather sitting at the Fed. They sit passive and inert because banks must hold these reserves as HQLA to meet LCR requirements.

Pozsar goes on to conclude that the new requirements imply "the need for a big Fed balance sheet for a long time to come" (ibid., p. 2), if not forever (ibid., p. 9). "There is no turning back," he adds, "to the old days where reserves were scarce. The LCR does not allow that. . . . Big is necessary. It is the future. Get over it." (ibid., p. 12).

But is it true that the LCR "does not allow" banks to get away with modest quantities of excess reserves? It isn't. While such reserves qualify as HQLAs, and, specifically, as the highest quality "Tier 1" HQLAs, so do U.S. Treasury securities, Ginnie Mae mortgage-backed securities (MBS), non-GSE agency debt, and, since October 2014, deposits at the Fed's Term Deposit Facility. Furthermore, up to 40 percent of banks' HQLAs may consist of "Tier 2" assets, which include other GSE securities, certain corporate bonds, and qualifying common stock. In short, banks might, in principle, meet their LCR requirements without holding any excess reserves at all. It turns out that in claiming that banks are now "required" to hold immense quantities of excess reserves to meet their LCR requirements, what Pozsar really means is that they *prefer* to meet the requirements that way *given* what those reserves have been yielding relative to other HQLAs! Cumberland Advisors' David Kotok (2016), in an article praising and elaborating on Pozsar's arguments, makes this perfectly clear:

The LCR requirement is met by the election of the commercial bank. Each bank, pricing its available alternatives, determines how to comply. . . . [T]he current worldwide pricing of alternatives favors the use of reserve deposits at the Fed. That explains why about half of the excess reserves at the Fed are placed there by U.S. subsidiaries of foreign banks. Those foreign-owned deposits meet LCR. At the same time those banks are earning 50 bps[31] paid in U.S. dollars instead of paying 40 bps in euro. That 90-bps spread is serious money and may be changing agents' behavior.

Changing behavior indeed. A recent study by several Fed economists, using standard portfolio theory and data for the 2012-2016 period, finds that even allowing that Treasuries are somewhat riskier than reserves, large U.S. banks "should not want to hold any amount of the risk-free asset—reserve balances—to satisfy HQLA" (Ihrig et al. 2017, p. 15). That finding is, moreover, robust for all values (1 being the lowest and 10 the highest) of their model's risk-intolerance parameter. A follow-up analysis, using the longer 2001–2016 sample period to allow for greater volatility of asset returns, still found Treasuries and GSE MBS dominating reserves for modest (<5) values of the risk-intolerance parameter, and this despite the counterfactual assumption of an IOER rate set equal to the effective fed funds rate prior to 2008. Finally, for smaller values of risk intolerance, even a small change in the IOER rate might result in a substantial change in banks' demand for excess reserves. If, for example, the risk-intolerance parameter has a value of 3, a 25-basis-point reduction in the IOER rate would, all else equal, reduce excess reserves' share of HQLAs "by about 10 percentage points," while increasing that of Treasury securities by the same amount (ibid, p. 17). Overall, these findings

---

[31] This was written on June 9, 2016.

suggest that IOER has contributed substantially to banks' use of excess reserve balances to meet their LCR requirements.[32]

Norway's experience, finally, in moving from a floor system to a "quota" system, where bank reserve balances held in excess of preassigned limits were compensated not at Norges Bank's policy rate but at that rate minus 100 basis points, confirms predictions such as those just considered. Indeed, several Norwegian banks complained that the switch made it costlier to satisfy their LCR requirements by compelling them to "seek other Level 1 assets as an alternative" to deposits at Norges Bank (Norges Bank 2014, pp. 21–22). To its credit, Norges Bank replied that "enabling banks to meet regulatory requirements at the lowest possible costs is not a concern [it] takes into account in its liquidity management" (Norges Bank 2014, p. 22).

Reserve Demand and Opportunity Cost

Final proof, should it be needed, of the bearing of IOER on banks' willingness to accumulate excess reserves comes from consideration of how that willingness has varied with changes in the relationship between the IOER rate and corresponding market rates. If banks' demand for excess reserves is driven by the yield on such reserves compared to that on other assets, then the ratio of excess reserves to total bank assets should vary with

---

[32] According to Ihrig et al. (2017, p. 12), at the end of 2014, when the requirements were about to be implemented, the excess reserves of banks subject to them were sufficient to satisfy 45 percent of the requirements. Since then, that share has fallen to about 36 percent. Excess reserve balances' share of total HQLAs also varies considerably from bank to bank. Of eight of the largest bank holding companies, reserves' HQLA share was 20 percent or less, whereas for others it was above 50 percent (ibid., pp. 18–19). Both the large holdings and the variations almost certainly reflect the degree to which reserves used to satisfy LCR requirements have been borrowed overnight from GSEs, as part of the fed funds arbitrage discussed previously.

Figure 7.8: Cash (Reserve) Share of U.S. Bank Assets and LIBOR-IOER Spread

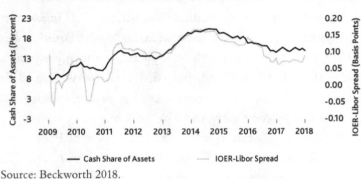

Source: Beckworth 2018.

the difference between the IOER rate and comparable short-term market rates, such as the overnight LIBOR rate. A recent study by David Beckworth (2018) shows that this has indeed been the case. As Figure 7.8 shows, for U.S. banks as a whole, the two values are closely correlated, with $R^2 = 77.24$. As might be expected, the relationship for foreign banks, shown in Figure 7.9, is even stronger, with $R^2 = 82.04$ percent.

Figure 7.9: Cash (Reserve) Share of Foreign Bank Assets and LIBOR-IOER Spread

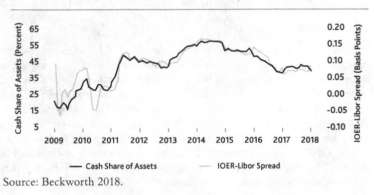

Source: Beckworth 2018.

THE FLOOR SYSTEM AND RESERVE HOARDING   69

A multiple regression analysis, also performed by Beckworth, with reserves' share of banks' total assets as its dependent variable and the IOER–LIBOR spread as well as several control variables as its independent variables, also shows the spread to be highly significant, both statistically (at the 1 percent significance level) and economically, with spread coefficients ranging from .094 for small domestic banks to .554 for larger ones to just shy of 2 for foreign bank branches. These findings once again agree with our understanding that larger U.S. banks stood to profit more by acquiring reserves than small ones could, and that foreign bank branches profited most of all.

8

THE FLOOR SYSTEM AND RETAIL LENDING

Lending Before and Since the Crisis

Between the first week of October, when it reached its precrisis peak, and the third week of March 2009, when it reached its postcrisis nadir, overall U.S. commercial bank lending fell from over $7.25 trillion to about $6.5 trillion—a decline of $1.25 trillion. As Figure 8.1 shows, although reduced real estate lending accounted for the greatest part of this decline, other kinds of lending, including business lending, also fell sharply.

Although lending has since recovered to a considerable extent, at least relative to its presubprime boom trend, that recovery was painfully slow. It also masks an enduring and substantial postcrisis decline in the ratio of overall bank lending ("loans and leases") to total bank deposits. As Figure 8.2 shows, total bank lending tended to match total bank deposits in the years leading to the crisis. As Céline Choulet (2015, p. 5) explains, that close relationship

> stems from the specific characteristics of financing via bank loans: when a bank grants a loan, it creates money by crediting its customer's account. This deposit may 'travel' towards a current account held by the customer of a different bank (e.g., when a customer buys a car from the customer of another bank), but at the aggregate level, loans and deposits outstanding remain in balance.

Figure 8.1: Commercial Bank Lending, 1996–2017

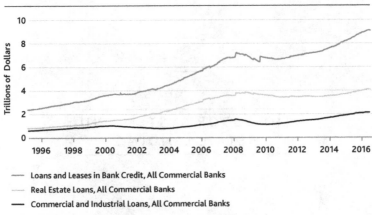

— Loans and Leases in Bank Credit, All Commercial Banks
--- Real Estate Loans, All Commercial Banks
— Commercial and Industrial Loans, All Commercial Banks

Source: Federal Reserve Bank of St. Louis FRED Database.

The Fed's resort to above-market IOER has, however, caused that traditional balance to break down, with loans declining to about 80 percent of deposits and bank reserves increasing from trivial levels to 20 percent of bank deposits. In short, as a matter of simple balance-sheet arithmetic, the rise in banks' holdings

Figure 8.2: Commercial Bank Deposits, Loans, and Reserve Balances, 2006–2017

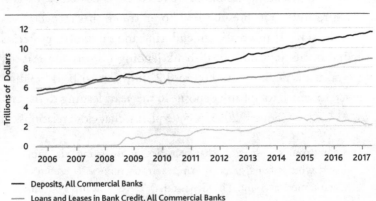

— Deposits, All Commercial Banks
— Loans and Leases in Bank Credit, All Commercial Banks
--- Total Reserve Balances Maintained with Federal Reserve Banks

Source: Federal Reserve Bank of St. Louis FRED Database.

of excess reserves has gone hand-in-hand with a corresponding overall decline in bank lending.

The Direct Influence of IOER on Bank Lending

But does it follow that IOER was to blame for the decline in retail bank lending as a share of bank deposits? According to Todd Keister, one of the architects of the Fed's floor system (2018, p. 5), it doesn't:

> There is a tendency at times to view the large quantity of reserves held by banks as an indication that these banks are not lending as much to businesses and consumers as they otherwise could. This view, however, is based on a fallacy of composition. While an individual bank can choose to lend out its reserves, the same is not true of the banking system as a whole. The total quantity of reserves in the banking system is determined almost entirely by the Fed's actions—how many securities it holds in its portfolio. Actions taken by individual banks change the distribution of reserves across banks, but do not change the total quantity of reserves in the banking system.
>
> Moreover . . . when the Fed creates reserves by purchasing securities from the public, this action also automatically creates bank deposits for the individuals or institutions selling the securities. As a result, both the assets and the liabilities of the banking system increase. The reserves that banks hold are not displacing other assets on their balance sheets, like loans to businesses or consumers; these reserves are, in general, held in addition to banks' other assets. In other words, the Fed's creation of a large supply of reserves does not restrict banks' ability or incentive to lend funds to businesses and consumers.

But the misunderstanding here is Keister's. First, as we saw earlier, although bankers' actions don't determine the quantity of *reserves* in the banking system, they do determine the quantity of *excess reserves* in the system. Banks can either elect to accumulate such reserves or not, depending on reserves' perceived advantages compared to those of other assets they might acquire. If they choose not to accumulate reserves, their actions aimed at achieving and maintaining the portfolios they prefer will ultimately cause the quantity of reservable deposits to grow, in turn causing former excess reserves to be converted into required reserves.

Second, although central banks can create nominal reserves "out of thin air," as it were, increasing the stock of such reserves effortlessly, they cannot effortlessly increase an economy's real supply of savings. When banks elect to accumulate excess reserves in response to the Fed's creation of additional nominal reserves, because they've been encouraged to do so by a relatively attractive IOER rate or for any other reason, real savings are directed toward the Fed, and thence toward those whose assets the Fed itself purchases, leaving that many fewer such savings for other prospective borrowers. In other words, there ain't no such thing as a free liquidity lunch.

Some other experts have insisted that IOER rates have been too low, compared to the rates on commercial bank loans, to have had more than a minor influence on bank lending. Ben Bernanke and Donald Kohn (2016) seem to imply as much in observing that during the long interval when the IOER rate stood at 25 basis points, "the only potential loans that would have been affected by the Fed's payment of interest [on reserves] are those with risk-adjusted short-term returns between precisely zero and one-quarter percent."

But Bernanke and Kohn's claim begs the question. As we've seen, the growth in banks' excess reserve holdings was not an inevitable response to growth in the Fed's balance sheet. Banks are always materially capable of reducing their excess reserve holdings, collectively as well as individually, by either making loans or by buying securities. Doing so increases both the total volume of bank deposits and the reserves legally required to back them. It follows that the existence of substantial excess reserve balances is *ipso-facto* proof that the banks holding those reserves considered them more desirable than *any* other assets they might have acquired instead, including bank loans. Moreover, since commercial banks generally hold relatively few financial assets apart from loans, it follows that the observed increase in such banks' excess reserve holdings had to come mainly at the expense of so much bank lending.

But can there really have been *trillions* of dollars of "potential loans" having "risk-adjusted short-term returns between precisely zero and one-quarter percent"? Perhaps not. But contrary to what Bernanke and Kohn claim, it wasn't merely such loans that banks would have been inclined to sacrifice. Instead, because reserves are not only risk-free but practically costless to acquire and service, they would have been willing to sacrifice any potential loans bearing a return of between zero and 25 basis points, allowing not just for risk *but also for the noninterest expenses, including balance-sheet costs, of lending.*

Nor is it hard to imagine banks, or certain banks, having the potential to make trillions of dollars of such loans. Because rates paid on most bank deposits have been very low, if not zero, for most of the period when the IOER rate was set at 25 basis points, banks' net interest margins for that period supply a rough indication of their gross interest returns. As Figure 8.3 shows,

Figure 8.3: Net Interest Margins of U.S. and Euro Area Banks

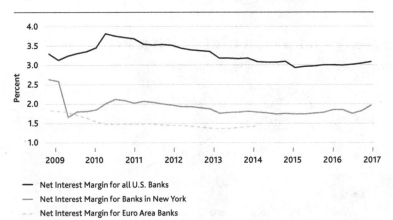

— Net Interest Margin for all U.S. Banks
— Net Interest Margin for Banks in New York
- - Net Interest Margin for Euro Area Banks

Source: Federal Financial Institutions Examination Council.

those returns have long tended to be lower for the very largest U.S. banks (proxied here by New York banks), and lower still for Euro area banks (branches of which hold substantial quantities of excess reserves), than they have been for U.S. commercial banks as a whole; the gap between small and large bank NIMs increased further since the crisis. Between August 2008 and mid-2015, NIMs of large (>$50 billion) U.S. banks fell 70 basis points, from about 330 basis points to about 280 basis points, mostly owing to declining yields on loans, while those of smaller banks declined only slightly (Covas, Razende, and Vojtech 2015). The NIMs of the very largest U.S. banks have fallen even lower. As we've seen, those banks, together with U.S. branches of foreign banks (which have still lower NIMs) have held the lion's share of outstanding excess reserves.

Even 150 basis points is many times 25 basis points. But we have still to take account of banks' allowances for default risk. Such allowances, known as loan loss provisions or loan impairment charges, further reduce the net return on bank loans (Noizet 2016). As Figure 8.4 shows, for U.S. banks as a whole, those provisions reached a peak of 3.7 percent of total bank assets at the beginning of 2010—a level comparable to U.S. banks net interest

Figure 8.4: Loan Loss Reserves of U.S. Banks, 2009–2017

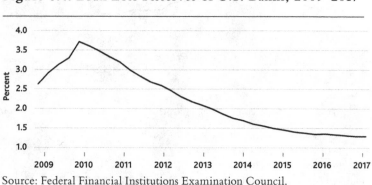

Source: Federal Financial Institutions Examination Council.

margins at the time—from which they've gradually fallen by roughly two-thirds. Even at this lower rate, loss reserves represent a substantial share of banks' concurrent net interest income.

Turning next to the noninterest expenses involved in making loans, these include costs of loan origination, underwriting, monitoring, and collections, as well as regulatory capital charges and other balance-sheet costs. All told, such costs can be quite substantial. According to Charles Wendel, a banking industry consultant, "it costs between $3,000 and $4,000 to obtain, set up, and monitor a small business loan of $100,000 or less" (Wendel 2015). In contrast, the sole cost of holding Fed balances consists of FDIC premiums assessed against them—and even that cost doesn't apply to most foreign bank branches.

Taking all the costs of lending into account, it's not difficult to understand how, in a situation where interest rates are generally quite low, even a modest IOER rate could make holding excess reserves seem more profitable to many banks than granting many potential loans, including ones paying considerably higher rates. For example, a bank that had the option in 2010 of making a small business loan to which it assigned a 5 percent default risk (a reasonable estimate at that time[33]), for which it would incur noninterest expenses equal to 4 percent of the loan's value, would have to charge more than 9.25 percent interest on the loan to top the 25 basis points it might earn by holding an equal sum in reserve balances.

Finally, it's important to bear in mind that in equilibrium, all of a bank's various assets should yield the same *marginal* net return. Because the demand schedule for bank loans is downward-sloping,

---

[33] According to PayNet's Small Business Default Index (SBDFI), small business loan default rates, which were about 3 percent just before the financial crisis, peaked at over 6 percent around 2009, and have since fallen to just under 2 percent.

the return on a bank's marginal loan will necessarily be lower than that on its loan portfolio as a whole. Consequently, the fact that bank's overall loan portfolios should yield returns exceeding the going IOER rate, even after allowing for both the riskiness of loans and the noninterest expenses of lending, is itself perfectly consistent with banks' finding it profitable to hold substantial quantities of excess reserves.

Figure 8.5 illustrates the last point. The downward-sloping line represents the marginal revenue schedule for loans confronting the banking system, while the light grey horizontal line represents the IOER rate, here assumed to be 100 basis points. For simplicity, I ignore banks' variable noninterest expenses altogether while assuming that the Fed adjusts the total stock of reserves to keep total bank deposits constant.

In that case, assuming they have $10 trillion in deposits at their disposal, the banks will collectively lend $8 trillion, while maintaining $2 trillion in excess reserves. But although the net return on the marginal loan is the same as the IOER rate, the banking system net interest margin, represented by the figure's horizontal black line, will necessarily be higher than the IOER rate. Reducing the IOER rate to zero, on the other hand, encourages

Figure 8.5: Bank Lending and IOER

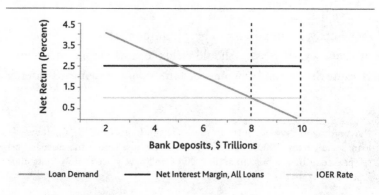

banks to lend 100 percent of their deposits, instead of holding any excess reserves.[34]

Excess Reserves and Bank Lending in Japan

Some may doubt that IOER accounts for U.S. banks' exceptional demand for excess reserves, and the associated decline in bank lending, because similar developments have been observed elsewhere where banks' reserve balances bore no interest. Of these cases Japan's is perhaps the most notorious. As Kazua Ogawa (2007, p. 241) observes, "Japanese banks have chronically held excess reserves since the late 1990s," with excess reserves tending to rise *pari passu* with the central bank's additions to the total reserve stock, just as happened in the United States after October 2008.

However, Ogawa also observes that Japan is no exception to the rule that "reserve supply does not necessarily automatically create a demand for reserves," and that Japan's banks, no less than U.S. banks, "have their own motives for excess reserves." The motives were, moreover, more or less the same in both cases.

---

[34] Alternatively, one can treat the horizontal axis in the diagram as representing real rather than nominal bank deposits, where changes in the IOER rate lead to changes in the deposit multiplier and therefore to proportional changes in both nominal bank deposits and the price level. A simple, formal model that yields results consistent with the diagram can be found in Appendix I. Using a more elaborate model, Martin, McAndrews, and Skeie (2013) reach similar conclusions. In particular, they find that "the key determinant of bank lending is the difference between the return on [bank] loans and the opportunity cost of making a loan," and that "banks lend up to the point where the marginal return on loans equals the return on holding reserves." They also show that once this point has been reached, further additions to the supply of bank reserves have no effect on bank lending; indeed, if banks' balance-sheet costs are high enough, an increase in reserves can even lead to a *decline* in bank lending. The last point has obvious implications for the likely effectiveness of the Fed's Large-Scale Asset purchase. Andolfatto (2015), using yet another model, also reaches quite similar conclusions, as do Dutkowsky and VanHoose (2017), whose model I discussed previously.

U.S. banks, as we've seen, accumulated excess reserves because the positive return on those reserves was greater than the still-positive (net) return on wholesale as well as some retail loans. Japanese banks, in contrast, began hoarding reserves long before the Bank of Japan began paying interest on reserves in November 2008—a month after the Fed did so.

But as the U.S. case itself demonstrates, what matters isn't the *absolute* IOER rate but how it compares to rates on alternative uses of bank funds. In Japan before November 2008, although the IOER rate was zero, the overnight uncollateralized call rate—Japan's equivalent to the fed funds rate—had itself fallen to zero, making reserves and call loans very close substitutes despite the fact that reserves bore no interest. Furthermore, as Figure 8.6 shows, the net interest margin of Japanese banks as a whole has been less than half—and often less than a third—that of larger (>$15 billion) U.S. banks. Finally, the fact that Japanese depositors became increasingly leery of bank failures in the 90s finally tipped the scale in favor of reserves, as Japanese banks gained a further incentive to bolster their precautionary balances.

Figure 8.6: Net Interest Margins of Japanese and Large (>$15B) U.S. Banks

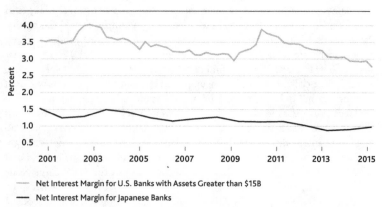

Source: Federal Reserve Bank of St. Louis FRED Database.

Figure 8.7: Bank of Japan Policy Rates, 1999–2009

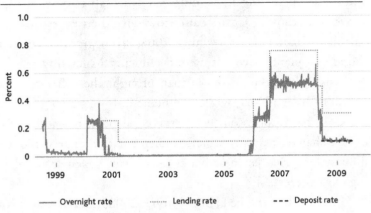

Source: Bowman, Gagnon, and Leahy 2010, p. 32.

As can be seen in Figures 8.7 and 8.8, reproduced from Bowman, Gagnon, and Leahy (2010, p. 33), during the days when the Bank of Japan (BOJ) paid no interest on banks' reserve balances, Japanese banks accumulated excess reserves only after March 2001, when the Bank of Japan, in initiating its Quantitative Easing Program, allowed the call rate itself to fall

Figure 8.8: Japanese Banks' Excess Reserves, 1999–2009

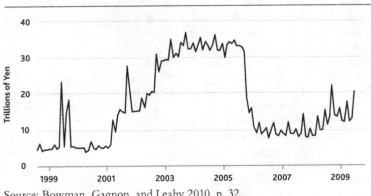

Source: Bowman, Gagnon, and Leahy 2010, p. 32.

to zero.[35] When the BOJ ended that program five years later, while also increasing its lending rate, the call rate again rose above zero, causing Japan's banks to reduce their excess reserve balances. Finally, in November 2008, by beginning another round of Quantitative Easing and reducing its lending rate to 30 basis points, the Bank of Japan brought the call rate back down 10 basis points, while simultaneously beginning to pay banks 10 basis points on their reserve balances. It was because of that change, marking Japan's implementation of an orthodox floor system, that Japanese banks once again began accumulating excess reserves.[36]

In short, like the Fed after October 2008, the Bank of Japan saw to it, intentionally or not, that Japanese banks' excess reserve balances rose and fell in lockstep with changes in the size of its balance sheet, which they would not have done had it maintained a positive spread between the call rate and the rate it paid on

---

[35] According to Bowman et al. (2011, p. 6), despite zero rates on BOJ deposits, banks preferred accumulating balances there to increasing their interbank deposits, which yielded small but still positive returns at the time, in part because Bank for International Settlements regulations considered BOJ deposits to be riskless, whereas those regulations required that 20 percent of interbank deposits be counted as risky assets against which capital had to be held.

[36] To pay interest on banks' reserve balances, the Bank of Japan established its Complementary Deposit Facility in October 2008. Although that facility was originally supposed to expire on March 16, 2009, it has since been made permanent. Interestingly, because banks were only allowed to place excess reserves at the facility, the BOJ paid interest on excess reserves only, and not on banks' required reserves. Japan's IOER rate remained positive until February 2016, when the Bank of Japan introduced a "three-tier" arrangement for Japanese banks' account balances with it, in which one tier pays a positive, one a zero, and one a negative interest rate. It's worth noting that, at levels intentionally kept between 10–30 trillion yen, Japanese banks' total negative or "Policy Rate" reserve balances are very small compared to their total ("Current Account") balances, which now exceed 360 trillion yen. Japan's set-up is therefore distinct from other multi-tier arrangements: the lowest IOR rate is applied to all reserve balances beyond some fixed threshold or exceeding banks' minimum reserve requirements.

excess reserves. According to Ogawa's estimates, had Japan's call rate been 25 basis points rather than zero after 2000, even with no improvement in Japanese banks' perceived financial health, banks' subsequent demand for excess reserves might have been reduced by as much as 70 percent (Ogawa 2007, p. 243).

Thanks to the Bank of Japan's strategy, and in agreement with our understanding that the influence of IOER on bank lending will be greatest where bank net interest margins are lowest, Japan's Quantitative Easing programs did little to boost lending by Japan's commercial banks. Indeed, according to Figure 8.9, showing year-on-year growth rates for Japanese bank lending since 1998, during those (shaded) periods in which the Bank of Japan was engaged in quantitative easing, lending by Japanese banks tended either to decline or to grow very slowly.

While it doesn't contradict the claim that IOER can be a crucial determinant of banks' willingness to accumulate excess reserves, Japan's experience does cast doubt on the suggestion that a U.S. IOER rate of zero would have sufficed after 2008 to keep banks there from hoarding excess reserves. Whether it would have depended on whether other U.S. short-term rates, the effective fed funds rate in particular, would have remained above zero

Figure 8.9: Growth Rate of Lending by Japanese Banks

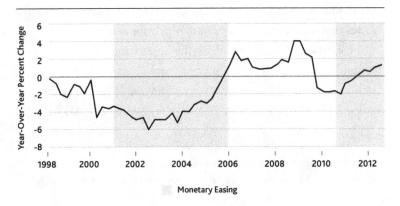

Monetary Easing

as banks disposed of reserves they no longer wanted. If not, nothing short of a *negative* IOER rate would have served to discourage banks from sitting on excess reserves by reestablishing a positive opportunity cost of reserve holding. Even so, a zero IOER rate would have supplied less of an inducement for reserve hoarding than a positive one. More importantly, as we shall see, by 2010 Fed officials were themselves convinced that had they returned the U.S. IOER rate to zero, the effective fed funds rate, despite falling further, would still have remained positive.

Bank Capital as a Constraint on Bank Lending

To insist that the Fed's floor system contributed to the post-Lehman decline in bank lending, especially as a share of total bank deposits, isn't to say that other developments played no part in that decline. Most obviously, a decline in overall loan *demand* was part of the story. But to suggest that it was this decline *rather than* IOER that mattered, as many in the banking industry seem inclined to do, is to erect a false dichotomy: if banks reduced their loans while increasing their reserves, they did so not simply because lending became less lucrative but because it became so *relative to the alternative of reserve hoarding*. Had it not been for IOER, banks would have been far less inclined to prefer reserves to low-yielding loans. IOER and reduced loan demand thus worked together, like the blades of a scissor, to discourage banks from lending.

A shortage of bank *capital*, on the other hand, might have prevented banks from increasing their loans despite the presence of both abundance of excess reserves and favorable lending opportunities. As Huberto Ennis and Alexander Wolman (2011) explain,

> As a readily available source of funding, high levels of reserves provide flexibility to a bank that is looking to expand its loan portfolio. However, loans (and risky securities) are associated with

higher capital requirements than reserves. A bank that is holding reserves but is facing a binding capital constraint is thus unlikely to engage in a sudden expansion of lending. As with deposits, raising capital quickly can be costly. For this reason, even a bank that holds a high level of excess reserves may not be able to take advantage of new lending (or investment) opportunities (p. 276).

However, in their own study of this possibility, Ennis and Wolman find that while many banks were indeed capital constrained during the Fed's "first wave of reserve increases," by the last quarter of 2009 bank capital had recovered to the point where, of $510 billion in reserves held by the biggest 100 banks, $485 billion were loanable. Barajas et al. (2010, p. 9) reach the same conclusion. By the end of 2011, finally, almost all of the reserves held by the same banks were loanable given existing capital requirements. In a separate study also looking at larger banks and BHCs, Jose Berrospide and Rochelle Edge (2010) likewise found that changes in BHCs' capital ratios had only modest effects on loan growth. Instead of worrying about capital, banks and BHCs seemed more concerned about things like loan demand and risk.[37]

Nor does capital seem to have significantly constrained lending at the opposite end of the banking spectrum, where banks must usually rely on retained earnings to build capital. According to Jim Wilkinson and Jon Christensson (2011, pp. 43, 46), who investigate lending by community banks in the Tenth Federal Reserve District between the start of 2001 and the end of 2009, programs established during the crisis for the purpose of placing funds into those banks' capital accounts did so little to boost that lending that it would have been "more effective for policymakers to give money directly to small businesses in the form of grants or loans."

---

[37] Unfortunately, Berrospide and Edge did not consider the possible influence of IOER.

9

THE FLOOR SYSTEM AND MONETARY POLICY

IOER and Tight Money in 2008–2009

Having addressed the bearing of the Fed's switch to a floor system on various sorts of bank lending, we're now equipped to consider how it influenced the course of the Great Recession and subsequent recovery. In brief—to anticipate what I hope to make clear in this chapter—the Fed's decision to implement a floor system and maintain a correspondingly high IOER rate contributed to both the recession itself and the slow pace of the subsequent recovery by serving as an instrument by which the Fed—whether wittingly or not—kept money too tight. This isn't to say that by merely keeping the IOER at zero, the Fed would have done all it could possibly have done to combat the recession. It simply means that an above zero rate didn't help.

Although there were clear signs of trouble in the subprime mortgage market starting in early 2007, the recession to which those troubles eventually led didn't officially begin until December 2007. As is true of any officially designated recession, it was heralded by a substantial decline in various measures of overall real economic activity, and particularly in the growth rate of real gross domestic product (GDP) that had been going on for several months.

Figure 9.1: Nominal and Real GDP Growth, 2001–2017

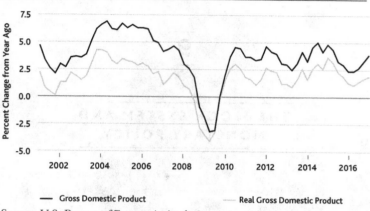

— Gross Domestic Product   — Real Gross Domestic Product

Source: U.S. Bureau of Economic Analysis.

As is typically though not necessarily the case, the recession also involved a similar but even sharper decline in *nominal* GDP, or total spending on goods and services. As can be seen in Figure 9.1, from a peak rate of over 7 percent during the boom, nominal GDP growth declined gradually to about 4.75 percent in the third quarter of 2007. It then fell precipitously, reaching a low just shy of *minus* 3.2 percent by the second quarter of 2009. And although the growth rate of spending recovered considerably over the next year, since mid-2010 it has never again reached 5 percent, and has often been below 3 percent. In short, overall spending never made up the ground it lost during the recession's first year.

While the connection between reduced spending and recession isn't inevitable, it's a strong one, for reasons that aren't difficult to grasp. A decline in overall spending means less money being offered in exchange for goods and services. If it's not to translate into reduced sales, and therefore into a decline not just in nominal but in *real* GDP, such a decline in spending has to be matched by a proportional decline in the prices of goods and services as measured by the GDP deflator. In that way, people could buy just as much despite spending less. In practice, because many prices are slow to adjust downward, a sharp and persistent decline in overall spending almost always spells recession.

The volume of overall spending itself depends on the quantity of money, however one chooses to measure it, and its turnover, or "velocity," which can be understood as an inverse measure of the public's demand to hold money balances, expressed as a share of their total earnings. The more money people seek to keep on hand, the lower its velocity, other things equal. As Figure 9.2 shows, although the velocity of the M2 money stock was growing at the beginning of 2006, by 2007 it was declining. That decline became increasingly rapid, especially after Lehman Brothers failed, so that by mid-2009, M2 velocity was more than 11 percent below its level a year before. Although the quantity of M2 was itself increasing, the increase fell persistently and increasingly short of what was needed to get spending to grow at its former rate again, let alone to make up for its previous decline.

Figure 9.2: M2 Stock and Velocity Growth, 2006–2015

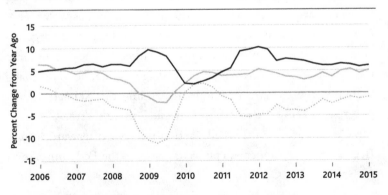

Source: Federal Reserve Bank of St. Louis FRED Database.

Instead, during the last quarter of 2008, the growth rate of overall spending fell steadily and eventually turned negative.

In light of these statistics, and allowing that the behavior of total spending is a more reliable indicator of the stance of monetary policy than that of any monetary aggregate, inflation rate, or interest rate,[38] it's clear in retrospect that monetary policy became increasingly tight during 2007 and early 2008, and that this overtightening became pronounced during the last quarter of 2008 and the first quarters of 2009. Taking a 5 percent spending growth rate to represent the precrisis long-run trend for the U.S. economy, it's equally clear that money remained too tight over the next several years to restore that spending growth rate, let alone make up for the fallen *level* of spending relative to where it would have been had spending not slowed down in the first place.

The especially severe overtightening that followed Lehman's failure reflected the FOMC's desire to maintain the 2 percent fed funds rate target then in effect. That target was, according to the committee's reckoning, consistent with meeting the Fed's inflation target, whereas anything lower risked surpassing it. Fearing that its emergency lending would prevent it from keeping the fed funds rate at 2 percent, the Fed sought permission, as we've seen, to start paying interest on banks' reserves to keep its emergency credit from spilling into the fed funds market. IOER thus became the chief instrument by which the Fed aggravated, however inadvertently, the collapse in nominal spending that was already in progress, making the recession that much more severe.

Commenting on the Fed's action not long afterward, David Beckworth (2008) went so far as to compare the Fed's mistake to

---

[38] In defense of this last claim, see Beckworth (2009), Sumner (2011, 2013) and Nunes (2014). Notwithstanding what low interest rates and other indicators may suggest, a collapse of overall spending is, *ipso facto*, proof that money is in short supply, and that monetary policy is therefore excessively tight.

the one it made in 1936–1937.[39] Some years later Scott Sumner (2017), having the advantage of hindsight, reached a verdict that was hardly less damning. "The decision to adopt IOR," Sumner wrote, "helped to *prevent* the Fed from achieving its policy goals, by making the Great Recession more severe than otherwise." He continued,

> The world would be a better place today if the Fed had never instituted its policy of IOR in 2008. I really don't see how anyone can seriously dispute this claim. If you want to dispute the claim, in what specific way did IOR make the world a better place? When the policy was adopted in 2008, the New York Fed explained it to the public as a contractionary policy. Can anyone seriously argue that the world would be worse off if monetary policy had been *less contractionary* in 2008–12? Why?

Fed officials were aware of the economy's deteriorating state as they prepared to begin paying banks to hold reserves: it was that deterioration, after all, that convinced them to finally reduce the federal funds rate target from 2 percent to 1.5 percent (see Figure 9.3) on October 8, 2008. Yet the Fed still went ahead, the very next day, with its IOER plan. Fed officials chose, in other words, to ease monetary policy *symbolically*, while taking steps to prevent the reserves it was creating from contributing to a further lowering of the effective funds rate. The FOMC's next and final rate cut under what still appeared to be, but was in fact no longer, its traditional monetary control regime, from 1.5 percent to 1 percent, was likewise largely symbolic, for by then the fed funds market, considered as a market for interbank lending, had ceased to function.

---

[39] In an action widely believed to have contributed to the "Roosevelt Recession" of 1937–38, Fed officials, fearing that a revival of bank lending would sponsor inflation, doubled banks' minimum reserve requirements between August 1936 and May 1937 in order to transform banks' then substantial excess reserves into required reserve balances.

Figure 9.3: Target and Effective Fed Funds Rate and
NGDP Growth, 2008–2009

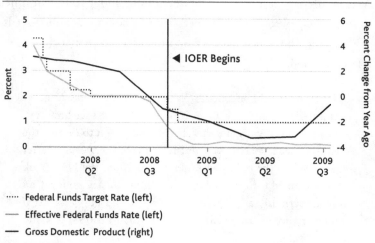

···· Federal Funds Target Rate (left)
— Effective Federal Funds Rate (left)
— Gross Domestic Product (right)

Source: Federal Reserve Bank of St. Louis FRED Database.

Thus far, at least, the Fed's experiment was proceeding according to plan. For despite the economy's ongoing decline, that plan called not for loosening monetary policy but for *avoiding* further loosening—and the revival of spending such loosening might have inspired—by preventing growth in the Fed's balance sheet from encouraging additional bank lending. Before the end of November 2008, however, the Fed had concluded that the economy needed to be stimulated after all. The trouble was that, with the Fed's new floor system in place, achieving a monetary stimulus was only barely possible in theory, and lamentably difficult in practice.

The Floor System and "Quantitative Easing"

As long as the Fed's floor system was in place, the Fed's asset purchases, no matter how large, would tend to lead to equal growth in banks' excess reserve holdings and, therefore, to very little growth in either bank deposits or monetary aggregates. That is,

IOER would have the same effect during the Fed's rounds of QE as it had beforehand, when the Fed's balance sheet was expanding, not as part of a deliberate monetary stimulus program but as the incidental consequence of its emergency lending.

If it's indeed true that "insanity is doing the same thing over and over again, but expecting different results," then one might be excused for wondering whether, in expecting extra bank reserves to stimulate the economy after 2008, using the same operating framework they relied upon to *prevent* extra reserves from stimulating the economy following Lehman's collapse, Fed officials were playing with a full deck. In fact, despite an almost 4.5-fold increase in the monetary base between December 2008 and December 2014, bank deposits grew only about 60 percent, while the inflation rate broached the 2 percent mark only fleetingly.[40] As Figure 9.4 shows, the growth in M2 was just as disappointing.[41]

---

[40] The Fed's three rounds of Large Scale Asset Purchases have informally come to be known since as QE1, QE2, and QE3. QE1, which was announced in November 2008, with purchases undertaken from March 2009 until June 2010, added $2.1 trillion, mainly in MBS, to the Fed's balance sheet. For QE2, which ran from November 2010 until June 2011, the Fed bought $600-billion worth of Treasury securities. QE3, finally, began in September 2012 and consisted of an open-ended program of securities purchases, starting with $40 billion in MBS per month and supplemented, beginning in December 2012, with monthly purchases of another $45 billion in long-term Treasury securities. In all, between March 2009 and October 2014, the Fed purchased securities worth not quite $4 trillion, or about 4.5 times its total assets just prior to the crisis.

[41] That M2 grew at all reflected the fact that banks largely participated in QE, not by trading their own security holdings for reserves but by acting as intermediaries on the part of their customers. Had QE merely swapped reserves for banks' own security holdings, it would have had no effect at all on total bank deposits or M2.

The Fed's QE experience was foreshadowed, albeit on a much smaller scale, by the Reserve Bank of New Zealand's mid-2006 decision to more than double that nation's monetary base, raising it between then and December 2006 from NZ$6 billion to NZ$14 billion while concurrently establishing a floor system by increasing its deposit rate "by 5 basis points five times between July and October 2006 for a total increase of 25 basis points" (Koning 2016)—enough to guarantee that banks would sit on their new reserves. The (big) difference

Figure 9.4: The Monetary Base and M2, 2006–2015

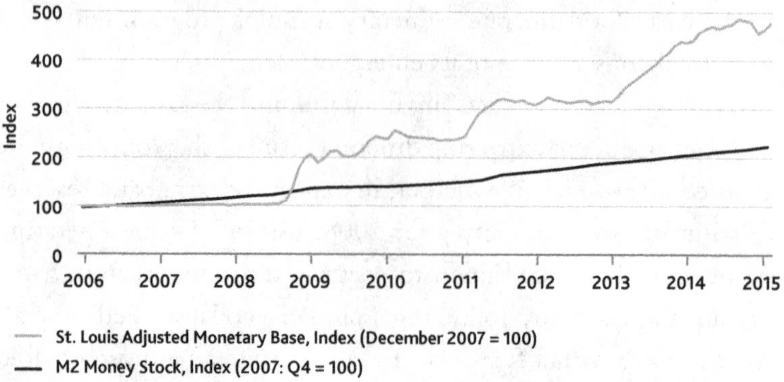

St. Louis Adjusted Monetary Base, Index (December 2007 = 100)
M2 Money Stock, Index (2007: Q4 = 100)

Source: Federal Reserve Bank of St. Louis FRED Database.

Although these outcomes took many commentators by surprise—including more than a few who feared that the Fed's asset purchases would lead to high, if not hyper, inflation[42]—they did so mainly because those commentators hadn't fully grasped the implications of the Fed's new operating framework. The simple truth was that by switching to a floor system in which excess reserves no longer carried a substantial opportunity cost, the Fed dramatically reduced the potency of its asset purchases by crashing the money multiplier (Williams 2012). As Figure 9.5 shows, the M2 base multiplier (the ratio of M2 to the monetary base), which had hovered between eight and nine prior to the implementation of IOER, has since fallen to half that value or less. Yet severe as that decline was, it was nothing compared to the astonishing decline in the bank reserves-to-deposits multiplier,

---

between this and the later U.S. episode is that New Zealand's central bank wasn't trying to achieve a macroeconomic stimulus. Instead, it merely wished to enhance the liquidity of New Zealand's banking system—a goal for which its policy was well suited.

[42] As exemplified by the signatories of an "Open Letter to Ben Bernanke" published in the *Wall Street Journal* on November 15, 2010 (Asness et al. 2010).

Figure 9.5: The Base-to-M2 Multiplier

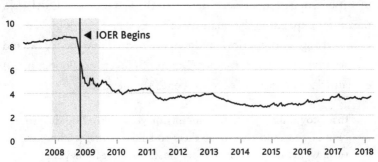

Note: Shaded area indicates recession
Source: Federal Reserve Bank of St. Louis FRED Database.

which fell from an average value of about 750 in months prior to September 2008 to around 10 from December 2008 onwards.[43]

But far from being *non compos mentis*, Fed officials were fully cognizant of these developments. They understood, furthermore, that the changes meant that Quantitative Easing, if it was to stimulate at all, could not do so by means of the usual multiplier-based monetary transmission mechanism. Some, including Bernanke himself, even

---

[43] To observe that the values of various money multipliers collapsed after September 2008 is not at all to suggest, as Martin Wolf (2014) and some other pundits have, that the very notion of a money multiplier is a "myth." Of course, there are no absolutely constant money multipliers. But while textbooks may occasionally assume fixed multipliers for convenience's sake, competent monetary economists have long understood that multipliers can vary, sometimes dramatically. Nor (despite what Mr. Wolf says) were matters any different in the days of the gold standard: in the United States during that time, for example, the variability of the base multiplier was a notorious source of concern. It's also incorrect to suggest, as some other writings (e.g., Martin, McAndrews, and Skeie 2013, p. 1) have, that the existence of a substantial multiplier depends upon the presence of minimum legal reserve requirements. On the contrary: as long as banks have a well-defined demand for either clearing balances or till money, eliminating reserve requirements, far from rendering the multiplier indeterminate, serves only to raise its value, other things equal. As long as required reserve and equilibrium currency-deposit ratios are less than one, the existence of a positive opportunity cost of reserve holding is both a necessary and a sufficient condition for the existence of a positive money multiplier.

went so far as to object to the expression "Quantitative Easing" because it suggested, misleadingly, that the Fed regarded LSAPs as a means for expanding the quantity of money, and for giving a boost thereby to spending, prices, and employment. "The theory behind quantitative easing," Bernanke (Board of Governors 2008c, p. 24) explained at the FOMC's December 2008 meeting, is

> that providing enormous amounts of very cheap liquidity to banks . . . would encourage them to lend and that lending, in turn, would increase the broader measures of the money supply, which in turn would raise prices and stimulate asset prices, and so on, and that would suffice to stimulate the economy. . . . I think that the verdict on quantitative easing is fairly negative. It didn't seem to have a great deal of effect, mostly because banks would not lend out the reserves that they were holding.

Just *why* "banks would not lend out the reserves that they were holding" Bernanke didn't say; nor did he so much as hint at the possibility that it may have had something to do with the Fed's decision to pay interest on those reserves—a policy originally adopted, let's not forget, to keep banks from "increasing the overall supply of credit to the economy" despite Fed-engineered additions to the total stock of bank reserves (Walter and Courtois 2009).

In any event, Bernanke and other Fed officials hoped that the Fed's asset purchases might instead influence the real economy through other channels. In particular, they appealed to the existence of a "portfolio balance" channel, in which changes in nominal (dollar) values, and nominal bank lending especially, played no essential part. Instead, the Fed's asset purchases were supposed to boost real economic activity by "reducing [credit] spreads and improving the functioning of private credit markets" (Bernanke 2009). Swapping bank reserves for long-term securities, in particular, was expected to promote investment by lowering long-term interest rates.

But whether there really is such a thing as a portfolio balance channel is a matter of considerable controversy. Just before he left the Fed, Bernanke, when asked how confident he was in QE's effectiveness, famously replied that "The problem with QE is it works in practice, but it doesn't work in theory" (quoted in Harding 2014). Though said in jest, there was more than a little truth in Bernanke's remark—at least in the last part of it. And Bernanke knew it. As a 2014 *Financial Times* article explains, according to theory that prevailed in the years leading up to the crisis,[44] if banks are indifferent between holding new excess reserves and trading them for other assets, Fed asset purchases

> should have no effects. All that happens is the central bank swaps one kind of government debt—money—for another kind of government debt, in the form of a long-term Treasury bond. That can only make any difference if investors have a strong preference for one kind of debt over the other (Harding 2014).

For the portfolio-balance channel to be relevant, it had to be the case, as Bernanke himself explained in his 2012 Jackson Hole speech, that "different classes of financial assets are *not* perfect substitutes in investors' portfolios" (Bernanke 2012; emphasis added).

Stephen Williamson (2017b, pp. 11–12), then of the St. Louis Fed, supplied what I believe to be the best assessment of dubious theoretical presuppositions of Quantitative Easing:

> A central bank is a financial intermediary. It borrows from a large set of people—those who hold the central bank's primary liabilities, i.e., currency and reserves. And the central bank lends to the government, private financial institutions and sometimes to private consumers.

---

[44] In particular, Eggertson and Woodward (2003).

Like private financial intermediaries, central banks transform assets in terms of maturity, liquidity, risk and rate of return. Therefore, the ability of a central bank to affect economic outcomes in a good way depends on its having an advantage relative to the private sector in intermediating assets.

When QE is conducted in a system flush with reserves, the central bank is typically transforming long-maturity assets into short-maturity reserves. The key question, if we compare this to how conventional monetary policy works, is what advantage the central bank might be exploiting in conducting such a transformation. That is not clear. . . . Therefore, from financial intermediation theory, it is not clear that QE should have any effect and it might actually be detrimental to the efficiency of the financial system.

But did QE at least work in practice, as Bernanke claimed it did? In the aforementioned Jackson Hole speech, Bernanke went on to refer to statistical evidence that the Fed's strategy had succeeded. But many other economists find this same evidence far from convincing. Williamson, for one, considers it "pretty sketchy":

For the most part, the empirical work consists of event studies—isolate an announcement window for a policy change, then look for movements in asset prices in response. There's also some regression evidence, but essentially nothing (as far as I know) in terms of structural econometric work, i.e. work that is explicit about the theory in a way that allows us to quantify the effects (Williamson 2017a; see also Williamson 2012 and Williamson 2017b, pp. 12–14).

The positive findings, furthermore, generally concern QE's effects on bond yields only, rather than on more important macroeconomic variables such as inflation and unemployment. As Mirco Balatti and his coauthors (2016, p. 3) quite properly observe, to conclude that QE was "effective" merely because it altered bond yields is to toy with the usual meaning of monetary policy effectiveness, by conflating a policy's success in influencing an intermediate policy target with its success in achieving ultimate policy goals. There are, after all, good reasons, as Charles Goodhart (2017) argues, for suspecting that the real implications of any interest-rate cut will depend on just *how* that cut has been achieved:

> One does not have to be a full-blown Monetarist . . . (and I am not), to feel that a condition whereby a 100 [basis point] cut in interest rates is accompanied by a 5 percent increase in broad money is likely to be much more expansionary than when the same cut in interest rates is matched by no such increase.

Since "[many] persons primarily access the financial scene via intermediaries," Goodhart continues, then "[i]f the transmission mechanism, via banks and other non-bank financial intermediaries, is seriously impaired, then so will be the efficacy of a given initial interest rate policy change, a point that most formal models miss" (ibid.).

According to Balatti et al. (2016, p. 5), while QE did indeed lower interest rates, it otherwise "struggled to propel the macroeconomy." St. Louis Fed economist Yi Wen (2014, pp. 1–2) likewise observes, with particular regard to the Fed's large-scale MBS purchases ("credit easing"), that while that policy "has had significant effects on lowering the real interest rate of private credit and raising asset prices . . . the picture on the real side of the economy looks gloomy, making it difficult to claim victory for [credit easing] despite 5 years in the making." According to Wen's analysis (ibid., p. 4), even if they'd been permanent, the Fed's MBS purchases "would have had little effect on aggregate output and employment." Even some top Fed officials who oversaw the Fed's QE operations were far from sanguine about their success. "I think it's fair to say," former Vice Chair Donald

Kohn remarked, that "although [LSAPs] were effective to some extent, people—even the Fed—were somewhat disappointed. It's been a slow recovery from a very deep recession" (quoted in Harding 2014).[45]

Several recent studies have, finally, cast doubt even upon the limited claim that Quantitative Easing reduced bond yields substantially. Angar Belke, Daniel Gros, and Thomas Osokowski (2017) look for evidence that the November 2008 announcement of QE1—which is usually supposed to have had a greater effect on bond yields than later QE announcements—led to a structural change in the relationship between U.S. and European bond yields. They find none. That can only be so, the authors conclude, for one of two reasons. One is that QE1 was in fact ineffective. The other is that it was so effective that it reduced foreign bond yields just as much as it reduced those of the agency debt and mortgage-backed securities that the Fed was about to purchase. QE proponents cannot, however, take too much comfort in the second possibility, because that possibility is also inconsistent with the portfolio-balance theory, "which is the dominant view of how QE is supposed to work" (ibid., p. 348).

According to Daniel Thornton (2017), although earlier event studies had informed a consensus view that QE lowered yields on 10-year Treasury bonds by about 100 basis points (Bhattarai and Neely 2016; Gagnon 2016), those studies fail to control adequately for non-QE news associated with the events they study, or to assess the statistical significance of the events' measured effects. According to Thornton's reckoning, of the 53 official FOMC announcements and statements by senior Fed officials that constituted the events examined by previous researchers, one alone—that of March 18, 2009—had both statistically significant effects, while being relatively untainted by non-QE related news that could also

---

[45] For a thorough evaluation of QE, see Thornton (2015).

have caused bond yields to decline (ibid, pp. 57–58). And even in that one instance, the announcement's effect on long-term yields "was so brief that it caused Yellen to rethink the effectiveness of the FOMC's QE policy" (ibid., p. 69).

Finally, Hamilton, Harris, and West (2018, abstract) also find, after controlling for events not taken into account by earlier studies, "that Fed actions and announcements were not a dominant determinant of 10-year yields and that whatever the initial impact of some Fed actions or announcements, the effects tended not to persist." They note that this finding is "in marked contrast to the effects of conventional policy in the pre-2008 era"—that is, before the Fed switched to a floor system (ibid., p. 39).[46]

Stimulus without IOER?

The most important question concerning the Fed's approach to postcrisis stimulus is not whether it was at all successful but whether another approach might have been better. In particular, what would have happened had the Fed dispensed with IOER, and the floor system it supported, while banks were still flush with reserves?

It happens that Fed officials themselves considered this very question as the Fed was deciding, in the summer of 2010, whether

---

[46] Remarking on these event-study criticisms, and on the Hamilton, Harris, and West study in particular, Joseph Gagnon observes (in personal correspondence) that they ignore other findings of positive portfolio-balance effects of QE based upon regression analysis, including one Hamilton himself coauthored with Jing Cynthia Wu (Hamilton and Wu 2012). But while several such studies report statistically significant QE effects, the discovered effects are not always either large or persistent. Thus Hamilton and Wu estimate that a $400 billion Fed purchase of long-term Treasuries would cause the interest rate on those securities to decline by just 13 basis points. Wright (2012) finds little persistence in QE effects. Using an estimated DSGE model, with particular respect to QE2, so do Chen, Cúrdia, and Ferrera (2012).

to renew the QE1 asset purchases it had tentatively ended that June. Then Fed economist Joseph Gagnon (2010) was among those who believed that the IOER rate should be lowered. In a July 2010 blog post, he wrote that "the Fed should lower the interest rate it pays on bank reserves to zero. This is a small step, as the current rate is only 0.25 percent, but there is no reason to pay banks more than the rate paid by the closest substitute, short-term Treasury bills."

Ultimately, however, the Fed chose to stand pat. As Ben Bernanke (2010b) reported in his Jackson Hole speech that August, having contemplated "reducing the IOER rate to, say, ten basis points or even to zero" as one of several alternatives to having the Fed buy more assets, he and his colleagues concluded that

> On the margin, a reduction in the IOER rate would provide banks with an incentive to increase their lending to nonfinancial borrowers or to participants in short-term money markets, reducing short-term interest rates further and possibly leading to some expansion in money and credit aggregates. However, under current circumstances, the effect of reducing the IOER rate on financial conditions in isolation would likely be relatively small. The federal funds rate is currently averaging between 15 and 20 basis points and would almost certainly remain positive after the reduction in the IOER rate. Cutting the IOER rate even to zero would be unlikely therefore to reduce the federal funds rate by more than 10 to 15 basis points. The effect on longer-term rates would probably be even less, although that effect would depend in part on the signal that market participants took from the action about the likely future course of policy.

These conclusions are striking for several reasons. They imply, first, that Bernanke and his colleagues no longer believed, if they ever did, that IOER alone stood in the way of having the fed funds rate decline to zero. If true, this meant that instead of merely allowing the economy to escape from its artificial, above-zero liquidity trap and straight into a natural, zero-lower-bound liquidity trap, abandoning IOER would have meant avoiding either sort of liquidity trap—and restoring the ordinary effectiveness of conventional monetary policies.

Second, given the prevailing circumstances, it is difficult to see why the Fed would resist a potentially helpful IOER rate reduction just because its anticipated benefits would be "relatively small." What, exactly, were the offsetting costs that made pursuing these small benefits unworthwhile? If there were none, why would the Fed resist a policy change that could achieve even the slightest gain? Is it possible that Fed officials were reluctant to revert to a zero IOER rate out of fear that by doing so they would appear to have regretted resorting to a positive IOER rate in the first place?[47]

Third, if one accepts Dutkowsky and VanHoose's (2017, p. 11) calculation that "banks would not have accumulated reserves so long as the effective federal funds rate itself remained at or above 6 basis points," the anticipated decline in the fed funds rate would almost certainly have left that rate high enough, with IOER = 0, to sponsor a switch back to the pre-2008 zero excess reserves regime. Because such a switch would have inspired banks to attempt to dispose of most of their excess reserves, the resulting increase in "lending to nonfinancial borrowers or to participants in short-term money markets," and corresponding "expansion in money and credit aggregates," would have been something other than "relatively small." Bernanke and his colleagues don't seem

---

[47] The last possibility shouldn't be dismissed too readily. As Allan Meltzer (2003, pp. 514–21) documents in his history of the Fed, Fed officials' unwillingness to admit policy errors has caused them to resist taking steps to correct such errors more than once in the past, most notably in May 1937, when they had reason to regret the reserve requirement increases they'd authorized over the course of the preceding nine months yet still persisted with a third planned increase.

to have considered the possibility that reducing the IOER rate below prevailing short-term rates might trigger a regime switch opposite that triggered by the Fed's original resort to IOER in October 2008. Instead, they appear to have only considered the immediate interest-rate effects of lowering the IOER rate, implicitly treating a low- or no-IOER alternative as just another way of achieving a portfolio balance effect, rather than as a way to put the Fed's traditional monetary transmission mechanism back in gear. By thinking so they underestimated the alternative policy's potential benefits.

Despite Bernanke's doubts, the possibility of lowering the IOER rate to zero remained a live one for some time. About a year after Bernanke's Jackson Hole remarks, in response to more bleak news about the pace of the recovery, the FOMC again considered lowering the IOER rate as one of three alternatives, the others being another round of QE and what would become known as "Operation Twist," for easing policy (Board of Governors 2011). Eventually the committee voted to stand pat until September 2011, when it finally chose to go ahead with Operation Twist—a program aimed at lowering long-term interest rates by swapping the Fed's Treasury bills and shorter-term Treasury notes for longer-term Treasury notes.

During the FOMC's July 31–August 1, 2012, meeting, held after the ECB had cut its own IOER ("deposit") rate to zero, some members again raised the possibility of lowering the IOER rate, but the possibility was again rejected (Board of Governors 2012b, p. 8). Although concerns such as those Bernanke had expressed earlier may have influenced these decisions, a more immediate concern—and one Wall Street voiced with great vigor—was that cutting the IOER rate would harm money-market funds by lowering yields on Treasury bills and other short-dated securities of the sort upon which those funds relied (ibid.; Robb 2012). To the extent that the concern was a valid one, it was also short-sighted, for although in attempting to dispose of excess reserves by acquiring other short-term assets banks might initially cause the yield on short-dated securities to decline, the revival of bank lending would ultimately have contributed to a general increase in spending and inflation, thereby raising equilibrium nominal interest rates.

Whatever the consequences of a lowered IOER rate for the money-market funds, the relevant question for policymakers should have been whether lowering the IOER rate would have helped the U.S. economy as a whole. Finadium's Jonathan Cooper (2012) believes it would have, and that for that reason the Fed made a mistake by not following the example the ECB set by cutting its own deposit rate in June 2012:

> If IOER went back to what it [sic] was originally intended—a rate pegged at below where the Fed Funds rate actually cleared in the market—it might be a first step toward banks thinking more clearly about how to put their cash to work, restore Fed Funds credibility as a market benchmark, and allow the Fed to start to get out of the box they've painted themselves into.

To see why, consider again our diagram representing the influence of IOER on bank lending, reproduced here as Figure 9.6.

Figure 9.6: Bank Lending and IOER

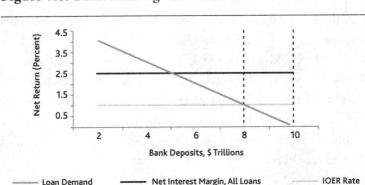

The Fed's assessment mainly takes account of the movement along the given, downward-sloping loan demand schedule associated with a reduction in the IOER rate: as the IOER rate declines from 1 percent to zero, the quantity of reserves demanded also declines, while the quantity of lending increases by a like amount—in this case, from $8 trillion to $10 trillion. But that change represents an equilibrium only if one assumes that the Fed *withdraws* $2 trillion in reserves from the banking system. Otherwise the banks will dispose of those same unwanted reserves by exchanging them for other interest-yielding assets, and they will continue doing so until deposits have grown to the point at which the quantity of reserves demanded is again equal to the quantity supplied. The reserve-deposit multiplier would, in other words, be reinvigorated, at least to some extent, and that revival would in turn mean that the overall nominal volume of bank lending, instead of merely increasing to the extent implied by a movement down a fixed loan demand schedule, would increase further by virtue of a general increase in nominal magnitudes, including a corresponding rightward shift in the loan demand schedule.

To get some idea of how much even a partial revival of the money multiplier would have mattered, consider that over the decades prior to Lehman's failure, every dollar of base money supported between five and eight times as many dollars of bank lending, the higher figure having been reached just before the crash. In contrast, as Figure 9.7 shows, by June 2010, mainly thanks to IOER, the ratio had fallen to 3.38. Consequently, even assuming, very conservatively, a post-Lehman base-money-to-loans multiplier of 5, the elimination of interest payments on reserves in the summer of 2010 would have, other things equal, raised the equilibrium value of bank lending by a factor just shy of 1.5, or by over $3.2 trillion.

Figure 9.7: The Monetary Base and Bank Deposits and Loans, 2003–2011

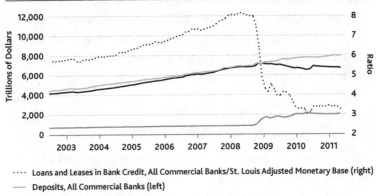

···· Loans and Leases in Bank Credit, All Commercial Banks/St. Louis Adjusted Monetary Base (right)
— Deposits, All Commercial Banks (left)
— Loans and Leases in Bank Credit, All Commercial Banks (left)
— St. Louis Adjusted Monetary Base (left)

Source: Federal Reserve Bank of St. Louis FRED Database.

Besides underestimating the extent to which ending IOER might boost bank lending, Bernanke (2010b) and his colleagues worried that it

> could lead short-term money markets such as the federal funds market to become much less liquid, as near-zero returns might induce many participants and market-makers to exit. In normal times the Fed relies heavily on a well-functioning federal funds market to implement monetary policy, so we would want to be careful not to do permanent damage to that market.

Here Fed officials' reasoning was not just incorrect but preposterous. As we saw in Chapter 4, if anything prevented the fed funds market from functioning as it had "in normal times," IOER was it! It's true that reducing the IOER rate to zero would have eliminated the arbitrage opportunity that was responsible for most of the fed funds lending that occurred while the Fed's floor system was in place. But as banks disposed of excess reserves they no longer wished to hold—bringing their holdings back to minimal levels—"normal" interbank lending would revive. In other words, what Fed officials were weighing as a potential cause of "damage" to the fed funds market was in fact the only sure means for restoring that market's robust health.

Stimulus at the Zero Bound?

Up till now I've assumed—in accordance with the Fed's own estimate at the time—that although eliminating IOER entirely would have caused the effective fed funds rate to decline, that rate would still have remained positive. That means that the change would have resulted in the re-establishment of the Fed's pre-October 2008 corridor-like system, in which banks were disinclined to hold substantial excess reserves. And that in turn would have meant a revival of the money multiplier and a corresponding, one-time increase in equilibrium bank lending, total spending, and inflation. Finally, the change would have moved the Fed's policy rate closer to its "neutral" or "natural" level, if not below that level, where a neutral (or "natural") federal funds rate "neither stimulates (speeds up, like pushing down the gas pedal on a car) nor restrains (slows down, like hitting the brakes) economic growth" (Federal Reserve Bank of San Francisco 2005).

Is it possible that the neutral fed funds rate circa 2010 was actually somewhere between 0 and 25 basis points? To judge by available estimates, it is, but only because that little 0-25 window falls within a much wider range of neutral rate estimates—not to mention a still wider range of minimum and maximum 95 percent confidence intervals around such estimates. As Figures 9.8 and 9.9 show, the mean estimates place the real neutral rate at

Figure 9.8: Range and Mean of Various Estimates of the Real Neutral Interest Rate, 1985–2015

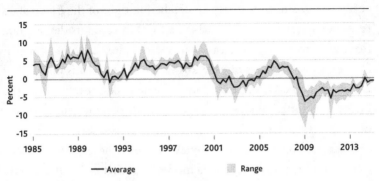

Source: Yellen 2015.

the time somewhere between 50 basis points and *minus* 600 basis points. Allowing for a target inflation rate of 2 percent makes for a range of nominal (steady-state) neutral rate estimates of between 250 and minus 400 basis points. Since—setting unconventional policy measures aside—policy was considered tight at the actual policy rate of 25 (or, if one prefers, 0-25) basis points, we might set aside the higher estimates. But we can't so easily set aside the lower ones.

Figure 9.9: Laubach and Williams (2015) Estimates of the Real Neutral Interest Rate, 1985–2015

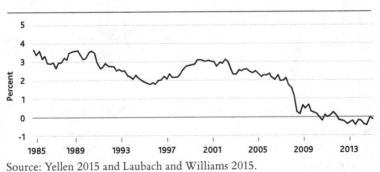

Source: Yellen 2015 and Laubach and Williams 2015.

The possibility that the Fed's IOER rate of 25 basis points alone stood in the way of its having avoided monetary overtightening may seem particularly far-fetched in light of the Eurozone's recent experience. In June 2014 the ECB lowered its deposit rate from zero to minus 10 basis points; since then it has lowered it further, to its value (as of June 2018) of minus 40 basis points. Yet Eurozone banks continued to accumulate excess reserves, and the Eurozone's inflation rate continues, as of this writing, to fall short of its target.

But the apparent inconsistency between the Eurozone experience and the possibility that a modestly positive U.S. IOER rate contributed to the recession in more than a trivial way is readily resolved by observing that according to available estimates, as shown in Figure 9.10, the Eurozone's natural rate of interest has been considerably lower than the U.S. rate. Those estimates suggest as well that natural rates have been falling since the crisis. It's entirely possible, therefore, that simply ending interest payments on reserves would have sufficed to avoid monetary overtightening

Figure 9.10: Natural Rate Estimates for the Eurozone (left) and the United States (right)

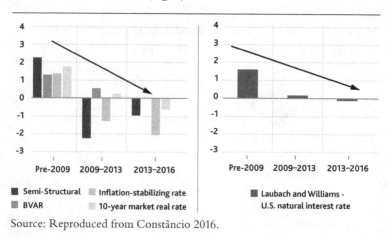

Source: Reproduced from Constâncio 2016.

in the United States between 2008 and 2015, notwithstanding that an IOER rate of minus 40 basis points didn't have that consequence in Europe more recently.

Suppose, though, that the neutral or natural value of the federal funds rate consistent with 2 percent inflation would in fact have been negative. In that case, eliminating IOER could at best have allowed the effective fed funds rate to fall to its zero lower bound, at which point banks would once again have been inclined to hoard reserves because they'd gain nothing lending. Would that in turn have meant the end of any potential stimulus, save that associated with the one-time 25-point decline in the IOER rate, and whatever might be achieved by means of extraordinarily large asset purchases?

Had the Fed's choice been between continuing to pay interest on reserves while resorting to large-scale asset purchases, or merely adhering to a conventional Taylor Rule—as it had, roughly speaking, throughout the Great Moderation—the answer might be yes. However, there were other options, including alternative interest-rate feedback rules. A number of studies employing several different models suggest that relatively modest departures from the conventional Taylor Rule would have allowed the Fed to achieve its macroeconomic objectives, despite the zero lower bound, and to have done so without dramatically increasing the size of its balance sheet. In every case the solutions consist of very similar "history-dependent" modifications to the Taylor Rule, with such forward guidance as those modifications imply.

In one of the earlier studies, David Reifschneider and John Williams (2000, p. 957) showed, using the Fed's own FRB/US model—a large-scale open-economy model that's been at use there since 1996—that the Fed might overcome the zero bound problem using a rule that makes up for periods in which the Taylor Rule calls for a negative policy rate by systematically keeping the funds rate at zero for an extended period to compensate for a "backlog"

Figure 9.11: Standard and Modified Taylor Rule Rate
Settings for Binding Zero Bound

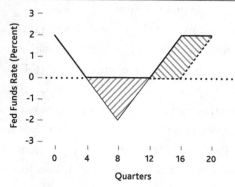

Source: Reproduced from Reifschneider and Williams 2000, p. 958.

of unachieved, negative rates.[48] As an example, Reifschneider and
Williams offer a situation in which, according to the standard Taylor
Rule, the Fed would have to reduce its policy rate to *minus* 2 percent
in order to avoid falling short of its 2 percent inflation target. In that
case, an alternative solution (shown in Figure 9.11) might be for the
Fed to commit to delay raising its policy target above zero until
sometime after the Taylor Rule itself would call for such an increase.

In their theoretical study of the optimal policy-rate path when
the zero lower bound is binding, Taehun Jung and his coauthors
(2005) reach conclusions quite similar to those of Reifschneider
and Williams. That optimal path, they conclude, "is characterized
by monetary policy inertia, in the sense that a zero-interest-rate
policy is continued for a while even after the natural rate of interest

---

[48] That Reifschneider and Williams reach this conclusion using the FRB/US
model is of special relevance, since that model, besides being the Fed's own
standard general equilibrium model of the U.S. economy, allows only for a
very orthodox monetary transmission mechanism, in which ordinary open
market operations are the Fed's sole instrument of monetary control, and those
operations influence broader money aggregates and inflation through "the
joint interaction of the money demand equation and the reserves multiplier"
(Reifschneider and Williams 2000, p. 947, n. 9).

becomes positive" (ibid, pp. 824–25). A central bank that sticks to such an "augmented" Taylor Rule

> is able to achieve higher expected inflation and lower long-term nominal interest rates in the periods when the natural rate of interest significantly deviates from a steady-state level, thereby stimulating aggregate demand in these [zero bound] periods. That is as if the central bank "borrows" future monetary easing in the periods when current monetary policy easing is already exhausted (ibid, p. 825).

Regarding other studies in the same spirit: using a New Keynesian model, Fernando Duarte and Anna Zabai (2015) show that the zero lower bound problem can be overcome by having the period of time for which the central bank commits to keep its policy rate "pegged at zero" depend positively on the extent to which it falls short of its inflation target. The extra zero-bound time commitment need not be very long to achieve its purpose. For example, if inflation falls short of its target by 2 percentage points, their model calls for a commitment to stay at zero for 2.8 years, as opposed to the 2.6 years that would be called for by a standard Taylor Rule. Siddhartha Chattopadhyay and Betty Daniel (2017) likewise show that a central bank can always achieve a desired degree of stimulus at the zero lower bound by adhering to a Taylor Rule modified to allow for both a time-varying inflation target and an optimally chosen, zero-bound exit date.

Finally, Hu McCulloch (2018, pp. 12–15) supplies an informal version of the same basic argument. Suppose, he says, that inflation is running at zero, or 2 percentage points below the Fed's inflation target, and that, according to a "benchmark" Taylor Rule, the Fed's optimal nominal funds rate target is minus 1 percent, implying an initial real fed funds rate that's 3 percentage points below the assumed natural real rate ($r^\star$) of 2 percent. Because it's constrained by the zero lower bound, the Fed, were it to simply commit to a zero rate for the usual six-month rate-setting period, would achieve only two-thirds of the needed stimulus. However, "[l]owering the nominal interest rate y($m0$) on loans of maturity $m0$ by Δi, while holding forward rates beyond $m0$ constant, reduces the cost of borrowing to any maturity beyond $m0$ by $m0\Delta i$." More concretely, and in plainer English, the Fed might still achieve the necessary stimulus by promising to keep the fed funds rate pegged at zero for at least nine weeks. "Doing this," McCulloch adds,

> with no direct disturbance to forward rates beyond 9 weeks would require the Open Market Desk to peg the interest rate on T-bills maturing within 9 weeks of the current FOMC meeting to [zero], and to hold them there until the next FOMC meeting. At that time, the FOMC would then be free to continue the stimulus by moving the peg out another 6 weeks, or to alter the strength of the stimulus in either direction (ibid.).

Though studies like these can hardly be said to leave us in no doubt concerning whether the Fed might have allowed reserve growth to drive the fed funds rate all the way to its zero lower bound, while nevertheless retaining some ability to stimulate the economy, they at least suggest that the possibility shouldn't have been dismissed lightly. They also suggest that the Fed's chosen alternative—a policy rate held above zero by means of interest on reserves—may well have been counterproductive, because it meant having an even bigger gap between the Fed's actual and ideal (negative) policy rate settings and a correspondingly greater need for offsetting forward guidance.

Positive, Zero, or Negative?

Although we've been assuming that, when short-term natural interest rates sink into negative territory, policy rates cannot follow them there, experience shows that this assumption isn't always valid. Indeed, not long after Bernanke and his fellow FOMC members had decided against lowering the Fed's IOER rate to zero in 2010, central bankers elsewhere began to contemplate not merely ceasing to pay above-zero interest on banks' reserve balances but switching to *negative* interest rates. On paper, at least, this was the "obvious" solution to the problem of a zero lower bound, though only in the sense that assuming a can opener is the obvious solution to the problem of opening a tin can. In practice, the technical and legal difficulties involved in making a switch to negative interest rates were far from trivial.[49] Yet many central banks, starting with Denmark's Nationalbank, have managed to do it. Denmark's example was quickly followed by the ECB. Eventually, the central banks of Switzerland, Sweden, Norway, Japan, Hungary, and Bulgaria joined in. Among them, the Danish and Swiss central banks plunged deepest, each having for a time set its deposit rate (that is, the rate paid on banks' deposit balances with it) at minus 75 basis points, or 100 basis points below the Fed's lowest IOER rate.

Suppose that instead of sticking to its positive-IOER floor system, the Fed had also chosen to combat the Great Recession by implementing a negative interest-rate policy (NIRP). Laurence Ball, Joseph Gagnon, Patrick Honohan, and Signe Krogstrup (2016) performed a counterfactual simulation for the period 2008 through 2015 in which they assumed that the Fed's policy rate, instead of following its actual path, was consistently set according to the Taylor Rule, even when that rule called for a negative rate.

According to their results, by early 2009 the Fed would have lowered the fed funds rate to about *minus* 6 percent, or 625 basis points lower than the actual IOER rate. That lower rate would in turn have caused unemployment to decline more rapidly, reducing the unemployment gap to just 1 percentage point, or half its actual value, by 2012. Inflation, on the other hand, would have been about a percentage point higher, briefly exceeding, instead

---

[49] Concerning the legal difficulties, see Zumbrun (2016).

of falling short of, the Fed's 2 percent target. "Because a faster recovery means that monetary conditions can normalize more quickly," the authors observe, their counterfactual federal funds rate "becomes positive in 2011, more than four years before the Fed actually increased the rate" (ibid., p. 11). Ball et al. (ibid., p. 23) also ask what difference it would have made had the Fed been limited to a negative rate of 2 percent or less. They find in that case that the fed funds rate, having fallen to the new *minus* 2 percent lower bound, would have remained there for just 10 quarters, and that "the unemployment rate would have been about 0.7 percentage points lower on average starting in 2010, for a cumulative reduction in the unemployment gap of about 4 percentage points." Inflation would also have been higher, though only slightly.

Such counterfactuals must be taken with a grain of salt, of course. Ball et al. never suggest that the Fed could actually have implemented a policy rate of minus 2 percent, let alone minus 6. Furthermore, it is far from clear whether by lowering its policy rate from zero to, say, minus 50 basis points, a central bank would achieve a degree of stimulus comparable to what it would achieve by lowering its policy rate from 50 basis points to zero. That commercial banks may find it difficult to charge negative reserve-balance rates in order to preserve their net interest margins as the IOER and wholesale rates fall below zero, and that their attempts to do so might only inspire the public to swap bank deposits for cash, are only two of the more well-discussed difficulties that can limit NIRP's overall effectiveness.[50]

---

[50] Eggertsson et al. (2017) claim that, because it can chip away at bank profits, NIRP may in some cases prove to be contractionary. Studies of Europe's experience with NIRP (Jobst and Lin 2016; Dell'Ariccia et al. 2017; Demiralp, Eisenschmidt, and Vlassopoulos 2017) conclude that while it may have had a slight adverse effect on bank profits, it has also contributed to modest credit and spending growth. According to Demiralp, Eisenschmidt, and Vlassopoulos (2017, p. 3), precisely because Eurozone banks can't easily pass negative reserve rates on to their customers, they have been especially inclined to respond to below-zero reductions in those rates by "reducing their excess liquidity to fund more loans."

Still the point remains that if a negative IOER rate was "optimal" in theory—that is, if it would have done the trick of hastening the recovery provided banks could pass the higher reserve tax on to their own depositors—a positive IOER rate can only have slowed the recovery down. That the Fed chose to press ahead with its positive-IOER floor system even as other central banks found it worthwhile to experiment with negative policy rates ought at the very least to raise doubts about the Fed's choice: if one of these opposite central bank gambits was prudent, the other almost certainly wasn't.

Canada's Counterexample

At the time of the crisis, the Bank of Canada operated a symmetrical corridor system, in which the Bank of Canada's lending rate ("Bank rate") served as the channel's upper bound, while the "deposit rate" it paid on banks' overnight balances—the counterpart of the Fed's IOER rate—served as its lower bound. Until April 21, 2009, these upper and lower bounds were respectively set at 25 basis points above and 25 points below the Bank's chosen overnight lending rate target. The Bank's IOER rate was therefore a below-market rate, by design as well as in fact. As Canadian banks weren't subject to any minimum reserve requirements, this arrangement encouraged them to keep their overnight reserves at a bare minimum, typically equal to about C$25 million.

As can be seen in Figure 9.12, between April 21, 2009, and June 1, 2010, in response to Canada's worsening recession, the Bank of Canada switched briefly to a floor system by setting both its target and its deposit rate at 25 basis points, thereby making banks indifferent between holding overnight balances and lending them. To drive the overnight rate to the floor, it provided banks with an additional C$3 billion in excess reserves, which they duly kept at the Bank's standing deposit facility. The Bank

Figure 9.12: Bank of Canada Policy Rates and Excess Reserves, 2008–2015

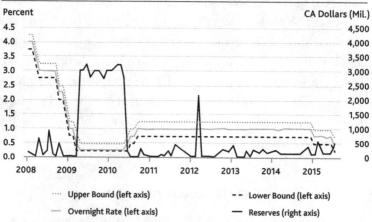

Source: Bank of Canada; Haver Analytics

also promised to keep the rate at 25 basis points until the second quarter of 2010, with the aim of achieving its inflation target. It thus used "forward guidance" to influence the public's interest-rate expectations (Woodford 2012, pp. 12–16). The policy having worked as intended, on June 1 the Bank withdrew the extra reserves it had supplied, returning to a corridor system by raising its overnight rate to a new target of 50 basis points, while keeping its deposit rate at 25 basis points (Bank of Canada 2010).

Were Fed officials right in thinking that continued reserve creation, coupled with above-market IOER, was a better way to stimulate economic activity than ending banks' extraordinary demand for reserves would have been? The Bank of Canada's experience supplies some reason for doubting it. Instead of moving to a permanent floor system, the Bank of Canada opted for a temporary one only, accompanied by an equally temporary boost to banks' excess reserve holdings. One might expect that a small and temporary boost to have been much less effective

Figure 9.13: Canadian and U.S. CPIs, 2008–2017

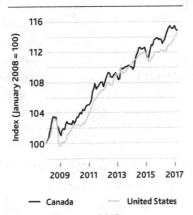

Source: Reproduced from Williamson 2017a.

Figure 9.14: Canadian and U.S. Real GDP, 2008–2017

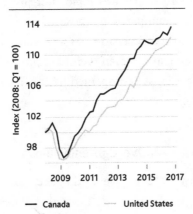

Source: Reproduced from Williamson 2017a.

in promoting Canada's recovery than the massive and sustained increase in U.S. banks' excess reserve holdings overseen by the Fed. Yet, if anything, the opposite was true. As Figures 9.13 and 9.14, reproduced from Stephen Williamson's (2017a) blog, show, Canada's price level and real GDP each recovered from their spring 2009 nadirs somewhat *more* rapidly than their U.S.

counterparts. "As an econometrician once told me," Williamson wryly observes in commenting on the figures,

> if I can't see it, it's probably not there. Sure, since Canada is small and highly integrated with the US economically, Fed policy will matter for Canadian economic performance. But if QE were so important, the fact that the US did it and Canada did not should make some observable difference for relative performance (ibid.).

Although the Canada-U.S. comparison suggests an alternative path U.S. policymakers might have taken, temporarily dropping their own IOER rate to zero and promising to keep it there for a definite span of time, giving bank reserves a temporary boost in the meantime, the comparison mustn't be pushed too far. Canada's recovery was rapid, not just compared to the U.S. recovery but compared to those of other G-7 economies. And although Canada's recession was severe, it avoided a domestic financial crisis, and, as Carmen Reinhart and Ken Rogoff (2009) have shown, recessions accompanied by financial crises generally tend to last longer.

An Overtightening Bias?

Beyond the slow U.S. recovery, the Fed's persistent postcrisis failure to reach its desired inflation target raises further doubts concerning the adequacy of its new operating system. This is especially so with respect to the period since January 2012, when, for the sake of keeping the public's inflation expectations "firmly anchored," the Fed announced an explicit inflation target, consisting of a 2 percent annual increase in the Personal Consumption Expenditure (PCE) index (Board of Governors 2012a).

In making that announcement, the Board of Governors declared that "the inflation rate over the longer run is primarily determined by monetary policy" (ibid.). That was certainly true under the Fed's traditional operating system, as is evident in the precrisis behavior of the PCE index, as shown in Figure 9.15 below. During that time, for better or worse, the Fed had no difficulty maintaining a PCE inflation rate just a little in excess of 2 percent, which was then, according to many, the Fed's implicit inflation target.[51] In contrast, between January 2012, when it announced its explicit PCE target, and the spring of 2018, with its new stuck-in-neutral operating system in place, inflation remained obstinately below its target level, despite a concurrent $1.25 trillion increase in banks' reserve balances. Allowing that conventional inflation measures overestimate inflation by failing to account adequately for prices of goods purchased online, which have been declining

Figure 9.15: Core PCE Inflation Rate and Bank Reserve Balances

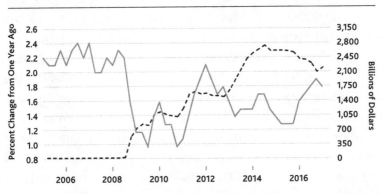

Source: U.S. Bureau of Economic Analysis; Federal Reserve Board of Governors.

---

[51] "For better or worse" because maintaining a steady inflation target at a time of rapid productivity growth meant tolerating unusually rapid NGDP growth, which may have contributed to the subprime bubble. See Borio and Lowe (2002).

especially rapidly (Cohen and Tankersley 2018), makes this persistent shortfall all the more worrisome.

As the *New York Times* reported recently, although "the direct cost of mildly undershooting the Fed's inflation target is low,"

> What is worrisome is not the direct damage, but the fact that the Fed has missed its (arbitrary) 2 percent target in the same direction—undershooting—year after year. . . . That in turn implies that the low-growth, low-inflation, low-interest rate economy since 2008 isn't going anywhere. This would prove especially damaging if the economy ran into some negative shock; a lack of Fed credibility could leave it less able to prevent a recession (Irwin 2017).

What has the floor system to do with the Fed's difficulty in reaching its inflation target? Of course, in any sort of operating system, an overly high policy rate setting will mean overtightening, with nominal variables falling short of their targets. The problem with a floor system is that it places an extra constraint on policy rate settings: the requirement that the IOER rate be at all times at least as high as the net return on other short-term assets. We've seen, furthermore, that even very modest changes in the relation between the Fed's IOER rate and other interest rates can suffice to trigger a switch, whether intentional or not, from a floor regime to a corridor system, with the troublesome unleashing of the reserve multiplier such a switch entails. For that reason, as Donald Dutkowsky and David VanHoose explain (2017, p. 11), it would only be prudent for the Fed to endeavor to keep its IOER rate well above any level that might risk an unplanned regime change.

Because the floor-system-preserving IOER constraint takes the form of an inequality, a central bank that's determined to maintain a floor system may be more likely to err on the side of monetary overtightening than one operating a corridor system.

Suppose, for example, that at some initial general level of market rates, the Fed's floor-system IOER setting allows it to consistently hit its inflation target. In that case, according to one criterion at least, the IOER rate may be said to be at its "neutral" or "natural" levels. Suppose as well that the difference between the IOER rate and other rates is just sufficient to satisfy the Friedman rule, according to which reserves must be at least as attractive as comparable (short-term and low-risk) assets.

Now imagine that the neutral real rate increases by 10 percent. To continue hitting its inflation target, the Fed must also raise the IOER rate by 10 percent. In contrast, to maintain its floor system it must raise the IOER rate by *no less* than 10 percent, because anything might inspire a disruptive multiplier revival. If, on the other hand, the neutral rate declines 10 percent, the Fed can maintain its floor system only if it lowers its IOER rate by *no more* than 10 percent, because in this case anything *lower* might revive the money multiplier. It's owing to this asymmetry, and to the possibility that the Fed would rather avoid the risk of undermining its floor system than that of overtightening, that a floor system may be said to pose a somewhat greater risk of excessively tight (but not excessively loose) policy.

Has the Fed's determination to keep its floor system intact actually caused it to err in recent years on the side of excessively tight money, by raising its policy rates more aggressively than underlying neutral rate increases warranted? The possibility is at least worth considering. Increases in the IOER rate, starting with that of December 2015, appear, at least on the surface, to have been more consistent with the objective of keeping the Fed's floor system in place than with that of achieving either robust spending growth or the Fed's inflation target. In any event, the risk that a commitment to it might lead to overly tight policy in the future should be considered another shortcoming of the Fed's postcrisis operating system.

10

THE FLOOR SYSTEM AND CREDIT ALLOCATION

Central Banking versus Commercial Banking

As we've seen, although the total quantity of Fed reserve balances is mainly a function of the size of the Fed's balance sheet, the quantity of *excess* reserves banks hold ultimately depends on banks' *demand* for such reserves, as influenced by their yield relative to other assets. Until it switched to a floor system, the Fed discouraged banks from holding excess reserves by confronting them with a substantial opportunity cost of doing so. The new system, in contrast, encourages banks to hold unlimited quantities of excess reserves and (what amounts to the same thing) to lend a correspondingly large part of the savings they secure from depositors to the Fed. As Hu McCulloch (2018, p. 3) puts it,

> The Fed in effect is now acting as a huge financial intermediary, borrowing reserve deposits from the banks at interest and lending them back to homeowners as mortgages or by transforming the maturity of the National Debt.

The Fed's increased role in financial intermediation is reflected in the fact, illustrated in Figure 8.2, that bank reserves, which until the recent crisis made up only a fraction of a percent of total

Figure 10.1: The Fed's Swollen Credit Footprint, 2008–2016

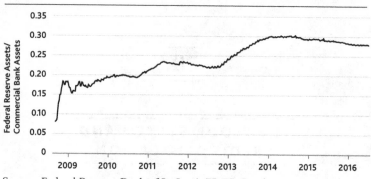

Source: Federal Reserve Bank of St. Louis FRED Database.

bank deposits, are now equal to a fifth of those deposits. Bank lending to businesses, farmers, and consumers, on the other hand, has gone from roughly matching total bank deposits to being equal to only four-fifths of those deposits. The Fed has thus made itself responsible not merely for regulating the nominal scale of deposit-based financial intermediation in the U.S. economy but for disposing of a substantial share of the public's savings. As Figure 10.1 shows, relative to the assets held by the entire U.S. commercial banking system, the Fed's holdings are now four times what they were before the crisis.

Were the Fed itself just another commercial bank, it might be expected to employ the public's savings at least as efficiently as commercial banks themselves might, by directing them to uses offering relatively high risk-adjusted returns.[52] But the Fed is a central, not a commercial, bank. As such, it was never intended to act as an efficient financial intermediary, whether by directly competing with commercial banks or by having them serve as mere agents to it, as they do when they hold substantial excess reserves.

---

[52] This isn't to say that commercial banks themselves always take appropriate account of risk. That implicit and explicit guarantees encourage at least some to occasionally engage in excessively risky lending is notorious.

Unlike commercial banks, central banks are supposed to secure macroeconomic stability and otherwise attend to the interests of the public at large, rather than those of their nominal owners.

The Fed's unique responsibilities have as their counterpart unique operating principles that differ greatly from those appropriate to commercial banks, including guidelines concerning both the sort of assets it should invest in and the extent of its overall involvement in credit allocation. A relatively recent statement of these guidelines can be found in a 2002 Federal Reserve System Study Group report on "Alternative Instruments for System Operations" (Board of Governors 2002). Among other things, the report states that as a public entity the Fed should "manage its portfolio to be adequately compensated for risks" while also maintaining "sufficient liquidity in its portfolio to conduct potentially large actions on short notice."

Until 1966 the Fed avoided taking on much risk by limiting its open market purchases to "bills only," meaning short-term Treasury securities. However, in that year Congress amended the Federal Reserve Act to temporarily allow the Fed to purchase any fully-guaranteed agency securities, and in 1968 that change was made permanent (Haltom and Sharp 2014).

The Fed was also supposed to "structure its portfolio and undertake its activities so as to minimize their effect on relative asset values and credit allocation within the private sector (Board of Governors 2002)." This last rule, the same report continues,

> is consistent with well-supported doctrines in the economics literature: In general, market price mechanisms allocate resources most effectively when undistorted by government actions, and market-directed resource allocation fosters long-run economic growth. The truth of these doctrines also has been borne out by much hard experience, both domestic and international, with varying levels of governmental intervention in the market process (pp. 1–2).

According to the FOMC's original guidelines concerning them, the Fed's agency security purchases also weren't "designed to support individual sectors of the market or to channel funds into issues of particular agencies" (Board of Governors 1971, p. 997).[53]

IOER and Financial Repression

Because the Fed's own portfolio choices are limited, and especially because those limits generally exclude lending to nonfinancial firms or individuals, it can't be expected to employ savings as efficiently or productively as commercial banks. It's therefore only reasonable that it should be expected to intrude as little as possible on "market-directed resource allocation" and, specifically, that it should avoid having banks hold unnecessarily large balances with it. Indeed, central banks that do otherwise have long been condemned for engaging in what economists call "financial repression," meaning practices that "prevent an economy's financial intermediaries . . . from functioning at their full capacity," thereby interfering with the efficient allocation of credit and impairing economic growth (Ito 2009, p. 430).[54]

---

[53] According to Renee Haltom and Robert Sharp (2014, pp. 6–7), during the December 2008 FOMC meeting held after QE1 had been announced, then Richmond Fed President Jeffrey Lacker observed that that plan appeared inconsistent with the guidelines in question, and also with the Fed's press release stating that the purchases were intended "to reduce the cost and increase the availability of credit for the purchases of houses, which in turn should support housing markets and foster improved conditions in financial markets more generally." In January 2009, when the FOMC voted to suspend the guidelines indefinitely, Lacker alone dissented (Appelbaum 2013).

[54] See also Roubini and Sala-i-Martin (1992), De Gregorio and Guidotti (1995), and Levine (1997). According to Ito (2009, p. 430), common examples of financially repressive policies include "interest-rate ceilings, liquidity ratio requirements, high bank reserve requirements, capital controls, restrictions on market entry into the financial sector, credit ceilings or restrictions on directions of credit allocation, and government ownership or domination of banks." Alper et al. (2016) offer a particularly insightful analysis and empirical investigation,

To put the matter plainly, suppose that by lending Tom $1000, the Fed creates the same quantity of additional reserve balances, and that by slightly raising the relative interest return on excess reserves, it raises banks' demand for such reserves by that same amount. In electing to holding those additional excess reserves, the banks in turn elect not to make a $1000 loan to Dick. The real resources Tom gets hold of thanks to the Fed having lent to him are, obviously, no longer available either to Dick or to anyone else. If Tom is less productive than Dick, every other Tom, Dick, and Harry suffers. This is true notwithstanding the fact that the Fed can create nominal reserves "out of thin air," that is, at little if any real cost to itself. Once again, there ain't no such thing as a free liquidity lunch.

That, at least, is the case assuming that there is no unemployment and that the economy is not already in a liquidity trap. If there's unemployment—if Tom and Dick are both on the skids—it may well be better to have the Fed direct resources to Tom than not, because doing so may put Tom back to work. But that's so only assuming that, because of a liquidity trap, even without interest on reserves, other banks would not have used the extra $1000 to get Dick gainfully employed. That is, it's only true assuming that fiscal stimulus alone, rather than monetary stimulus in the strict sense, is capable of promoting recovery. And even in that special case, once the recession ends, one would want to see the Fed's balance sheet shrink again, at least in real (or proportional) terms, to keep resources from being wasted.

---

using Turkish bank data, of the effects of minimum reserve requirements on bank lending, in which they conclude "that a 1 percentage point increase in the RR [Reserve Requirement] is associated with an increase of about 50 basis points in commercial loan rates" (ibid., p.12).

While high minimum reserve requirements and the use of relatively high IOER rates to induce banks to accumulate excess reserves both alter the direction of credit allocation, they also tend to enhance governments' seigniorage revenues, while high IOER rates may not serve that purpose.

As we've seen, by establishing a floor system and generating trillions of dollars in additional reserve balances, the Fed has increased the share of Fed-directed resource allocation, while reducing that of market-directed resource allocation to a correspondingly great extent. Instead of being offered by private-sector lenders to (mainly) private-sector borrowers, the real resources represented by commercial banks' excess reserve balances are channeled by the Fed toward the institutions that issued the securities it purchased during several rounds of Quantitative Easing.

While it's generally recognized that high mandatory reserve requirements are financially repressive, some may wonder whether making it worthwhile to banks to accumulate excess reserves can have similar consequences. If holding reserves pays more than other uses of funds, then isn't it also efficient for banks to hold reserves instead of acquiring other assets?

The answer is that it *would* be efficient *if* the Fed's relatively high IOER rates reflected its own capacity to employ funds more productively than private-market lenders. In fact, the Fed's ability to pay above-market IOER rates has been due not to its being an unusually efficient intermediary but to the seigniorage it earns on its noninterest-bearing notes and on noninterest-bearing balances kept with it, which it can use to cross-subsidize bank reserves. Furthermore, because the Fed doesn't practice mark-to-market accounting, it doesn't have to provide for unrealized portfolio losses. Consequently, it is able to finance relatively high IOER rates in part by assuming greater risks, including the substantial duration risk it took on by acquiring long-term Treasury and mortgage-backed securities. By using those high IOER rates to compete with private-sector borrowers for commercial bank funds, the Fed alters both the scope and the direction of bank-assisted financial intermediation. Although it's true that, by reducing the implicit tax on bank reserves and allowing banks in turn to offer higher deposit rates, paying interest on reserves can increase the overall demand for bank deposits and, therefore, the overall extent of bank-assisted intermediation, it also means having the Fed grab a larger share—and perhaps a *substantially* larger share—of bank-intermediated funds for itself.

To gain a more complete appreciation of the real consequences of above-market IOER rates on the one hand and high manda- tory reserve requirements on the other, suppose that instead of paying banks to hoard reserves, the Fed achieved a similarly high reserve ratio by imposing a continuously enforced 20 percent reserve requirement against all commercial bank deposits. Taken alone, that step would lead to a severe contraction in nominal bank lending and bank deposits and, ultimately, to a correspond- ing decline in prices. In the resulting equilibrium, the Fed's *real* asset holdings would have grown, in both absolute terms and rel- ative to commercial bank assets, by roughly the same extent as they have as a result of interest payments on reserves. Only in this case there would be no doubt concerning the "repression" involved, consisting of a reallocation of savings from commercial banks to the Fed and a corresponding shift from commercial bank lending to lending to issuers of the Fed-favored securities.

Because it calls for a substantial decline in prices, the scenario just described would be extremely disruptive. Suppose instead that rather than subject the economy to a severe deflation, the Fed accompanied its new 20 percent reserve requirement with a plan to expand its balance sheet just enough to allow banks to meet the new requirement without having to shrink their own balance sheets. Although the revised procedure would avoid deflation, it would, according to standard quantity-theory reasoning, result in the same long-run *real* outcomes as the one just described. That is, it would lead to a new steady-state that would be just as finan- cially repressive because it would involve an identical reduction in the (real) supply of bank credit.

The Fed's actual interest on reserves policy resembles this last alternative, the difference being its use of subsidized interest on reserve payments instead of high mandatory reserve requirements to boost banks' demand for reserves. That difference makes the interest on reserves alternative somewhat less financially repressive. Instead of exposing banks to a larger required reserve tax burden, it lowers that burden, allowing banks in turn to raise their deposit rates somewhat instead of having to reduce them as they must when they're compelled to hold more noninterest-bearing reserves. Interest on reserves therefore has both "income" and "substitution" effects on financial intermediation, where the first increases its overall extent and the second directs a larger share away from private borrowers and toward the Fed. An increased interest rate on both required and excess reserves will be financially repressive as long as the income effect is small relative to the substitution effect. Because the increase in banks' net interest income consists mainly if not solely of income earned on their (relatively modest) *required* reserve balances,[55] and most studies suggest that the demand for bank deposits is not very interest elastic,[56] that condition is very likely to be met.

Reserve Hoarding and the Productivity Slowdown

One of the most disconcerting features of the postcrisis recovery has been the "great productivity slowdown" that accompanied it. Although the slowdown started long before the crisis began,

---

[55] For a formal demonstration of this, see Dutkowsky and VanHoose (2017) who observe (ibid., p. 6): "On the one hand, an increase in the interest rate on reserves induces banks to substitute out of retail loans into excess reserves, reflected in the negative term. On the other hand, the rise in the interest rate on reserves increases revenue from *required* reserves. This prompts banks to demand more deposit funds and thereby allocate more of these funds to retail loans, as described by the positive term. Note that when the [required] reserve ratio equals zero, the positive term in the expression disappears. In that case, substitution, like the effect of the federal funds rate on retail loans, prevails."
[56] See, for example, Amal and Hannan (1999).

it became much more pronounced afterward. Between 2007 and 2017, labor productivity grew at an average annual rate of just 1.2 percent—far below the 2.3 percent average growth rate between 1947 and 2006; for most of the period since 2010, the growth rate has been just 0.6 percent (Kravis 2017; Sprague 2017). The growth rate of total (or "multi") factor productivity—the ratio of total output to the quantity of inputs of all sorts employed in making it—fell as well, from an average of 1.4 percent between 2000 and 2007 to one of only 0.5 percent between 2007 and 2017.

Many reasons have been offered for the slowdown, one of which is a deficient supply of bank credit. As the abstract to a recent IMF study (Duval, Hong, and Timmer 2017) puts it, "the combination of pre-existing firm-level financial fragilities and tightening credit conditions made an important contribution to the post-crisis productivity slowdown." San Francisco Fed economists Michael Redmond and Willem Van Zandweghe (2016, p. 41) consider a reduced postcrisis supply of credit the "primary suspect" in the postcrisis decline in U.S. total factor productivity, blaming it for having "prevented [established] firms from investing in innovations" and for making it harder for new firms to enter the market (ibid., p. 39).

The tightening of credit to which the above-mentioned studies refer is likely to be due, at least in part, to crisis-related fears and uncertainties, together with more stringent postcrisis bank regulation. Some of it can also be traced to novel postcrisis central bank operating frameworks, floor systems especially, that have reduced the flow of bank credit to business borrowers by boosting banks' demand for reserve balances. By encouraging banks to fund central bank balance sheets instead of making loans to businesses, these arrangements make it more difficult, other things being equal, for businesses to finance capital investment and R&D, both of which contribute to productivity.

Productivity is unlikely, on the other hand, to get boosted by the Fed's investment in Treasury and agency debt. As Robert Barro (2016, p. 6) observed, referring to the postcrisis increase in the Fed's balance sheet and credit footprint, "The dramatic rise in high-powered money was good for the Fed's profits (most of which went to the U.S. Treasury). However, none of this was likely to contribute to productivity growth." On the contrary: despite then Governor Jerome Powell's (2017) claim that "monetary policy . . . cannot reliably affect the long-run sustainable level of the economy's growth," by greatly increasing the size of its credit-intermediation footprint, the Fed has almost certainly adversely influenced U.S. economic growth.

Determining the approximate size of this adverse contribution is far from simple, in part because it means untangling the contribution of the Fed's re-direction of credit from that of other, including regulatory, credit-supply "frictions." The necessary research has yet to be undertaken. But given the Fed's long-standing precrisis policy of maintaining a small credit footprint, and the understanding of the advantages of private credit allocation upon which that policy rested, the burden of proof should surely be borne by those who maintain that the Fed's new operating system, with the much-enlarged Fed credit footprint it entails, has *not* contributed, or has contributed only insignificantly, to the productivity slump.[57]

---

[57] Silvia Merler (2018) surveys important recent research, mostly pertaining to countries other than the United States, concerning "The Financial Side of the Productivity Slowdown."

11

FISCAL CONSEQUENCES OF THE FLOOR SYSTEM

A floor system differs from any sort of corridor system, including the Fed's precrisis system, not only in its effects on the workings of monetary policy in the strict sense, or on credit allocation, but also in its broader fiscal implications. In particular, it differs in three respects. First, other things equal, a floor system results in lower Fed remittances to the Treasury than a more traditional operating framework. Second, whereas under its traditional operating system, the Fed never risked becoming insolvent, it does face such a risk, albeit perhaps a very slight one, under a floor system. Finally, whereas under its old framework the size of the Fed's balance sheet was a crucial determinant of its monetary policy stance, that's no longer so today. Instead, the size of the Fed's balance sheet must be decided by other considerations.

Treasury Remittances

The Federal Reserve's capacity to generate interest revenues in excess of its interest expense, and to do so even despite holding safe, short-term Treasury securities, rests upon its ability to pay below-market interest rates on its liabilities. Until the crisis, the Federal Reserve's liabilities, including both its circulating notes and its deposit balances, were noninterest-bearing. Consequently, whatever interest the Fed earns on its own asset holdings is interest free and clear of any associated interest expenses, and since it earns tens of billions of dollars in net interest income, while its operating expenses amount to several billion dollars only, the Fed faces practically no risk of becoming insolvent.[58] Whatever income the Fed earns beyond its operating expenses is first used to pay its statutory dividends and to fund its capital surplus. The rest is remitted to the Treasury. According to a recent GAO report (United States, Government Accountability Office 2017, p. 10), since the Fed was first established, the Treasury has received about 95 percent of its net earnings.

Compared to a corridor arrangement, where the IOER rate is set below the fed funds target rate, a floor system in which the Fed invests in short-term Treasury securities only reduces the Fed's remittances to the Treasury by the extra interest the Fed must pay on banks' *required* reserve balances only. This means that the revenue shortfall remains the same regardless of the quantity of *excess* reserves outstanding and any corresponding change in the size of the Fed's balance sheet, because, assuming that the "Friedman rule" is being satisfied, the Fed must pay out interest on those excess reserves at least equal to what it earns on the short-term, low-risk assets it funds using them. It must, in other words, pay the same rate that banks would earn were they to trade excess reserves for those same assets.

Because excess bank reserves may no longer be a source of net income under a floor system, it's at least conceivable that a central bank operating such a system might become insolvent—it's conceivable, in other words, that the discounted present value of its net earnings could fall below zero. For example, suppose

---

[58] The Fed also earns modest amounts of noninterest revenue from fees it charges depository institutions for various services. But under the rules of the 1980 Depository Institutions Deregulation and Monetary Control Act, those fees are only supposed to just cover the Fed's costs of supplying those services.

that the liabilities of a central bank operating with a floor system consist *exclusively* of bank reserve balances, and that it has no other sources of net revenue. In that case, a *sufficient* condition for the central bank to be insolvent is that its operating expenses are greater than zero! Any obligation to pay dividends or contribute to a surplus fund might also suffice.[59]

In practice, though, as can be seen in Figure 11.1, the Fed's floor system, far from rendering it insolvent, has allowed it to earn

Figure 11.1: Fed Remittances to the Treasury, 2001–2016

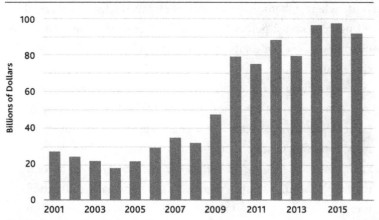

Source: Quarterly call report data.

---

[59] The Federal Reserve System's annual operating expenses for 2016 approached $6.68 billion. Until recently all Fed member banks received dividends equal to 6 percent of their paid-in capital. However, the Fixing America's Surface Transportation ("FAST") Act of 2015 reduced the dividend for banks with over $10 billion in assets to the lesser of the 10-year Treasury note rate or 6 percent. The FAST Act also placed a $10 billion cap on the Fed's surplus account.

In claiming that it is "perfectly feasible" for a central bank to pay interest on reserves according to the Friedman-rule policy "since the interest it must pay on its outstanding reserves is covered by the interest it earns on the assets it purchased when those reserves were created," Keister, Martin, and McAndrews (2015, p. 4) overlook central banks' noninterest expenses and obligations. They are right, on the other hand, in faulting Berentsen et al. (2014) for exaggerating the prospects for insolvency under a floor system by assuming, in their baseline analysis at least, that the central bank has liabilities, but no assets!

and remit to the Treasury more revenue than ever. There are three reasons for this. First, while the Fed now pays interest on banks' reserve balances and (through its ON-RRP program) on balances held by GSEs, it still doesn't pay any interest on its other liabilities, including outstanding Federal Reserve notes. Those notes therefore "effectively provide an interest-free loan to the Federal Reserve, which, given Federal Reserve remittance policies, implies they represent an interest-free loan to the Treasury" (Wall 2015).

Although currency now makes up only about one-third of the Fed's total liabilities, while bank reserves make up 60 percent, whereas before the crisis the respective figures were about 90 percent and 2 percent, the Fed's net earnings depend not on currency's *share* but on its total amount, which has almost doubled since August 2008.

A doubling of the outstanding stock of currency cannot, however, alone account for a near tripling of the Fed's Treasury remittances, especially considering the general postcrisis decline in interest rates, including yields on short-term Treasury securities. Nor can the vast post-2008 increase in banks' excess reserves alone account for it: as we've seen, that growth alone would normally cause the Fed's interest expenses to grow in step with its interest earnings. Instead, the difference is due to the Fed's having purchased long-term securities. Doing so allowed it to profit from the prevailing term premium, though only by taking on considerable interest-rate risk.

Indeed, if there is any serious risk that the Fed's floor system might render it insolvent, it arises from the possibility that, as a result of its attempts to profit in the short-run from increased bank excess reserve holdings by assuming more duration risk, it suffers losses large enough to wipe out the profits it earns on its noninterest-bearing liabilities. In that case, the Fed would face two possibilities: it might be recapitalized by the Treasury, or it might be compelled to abandon its floor system, with its implicit Friedman rule, and to resort to higher inflation as a means for

Figure 11.2: Projected Fed Losses

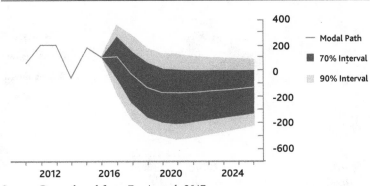

Source: Reproduced from Ferris et al. 2017.

increasing its monopoly profits (Bassetto and Messer 2013, p. 413; see also Del Negro and Sims 2015).

According to projections by Fed economists and others (e.g., Carpenter et al. 2013; Greenlaw et al. 2013; Del Negro and Sims 2015; Ferris et al. 2017; and Cavallo et al. 2018), the Fed's losses due to rising interest rates are likely to be modest compared to the present value of its future monopoly profits. Still, as Figure 11.2 shows, those losses are likely to be far from trivial. It's owing to them, not to the unwinding of its balance sheet, that the Fed expects its Treasury remittances, as shown in Figure 11.3, to decline substantially in the coming years.[60]

---

[60] Fed earnings projections are, furthermore, sensitive to assumptions made about future Treasury security term premiums. Cavallo et al.'s claim that a larger Fed balance sheet will ultimately mean increased Fed remittances to the Treasury, for example, rests on the assumption that term premiums will eventually rise to their historically positive values. If one assumes instead that the term premium, which has been trending downward for many years and is presently negative, will remain so in the future, the larger the Fed's balance sheet, the lower its Treasury remittances will be. That case of course amounts to a further argument for keeping the Fed as small as possible. (I thank Bill Nelson, Chief Economist and Head of Research at the Clearing House Association, for drawing my attention to this issue.)

Figure 11.3: Projected Fed Remittances to the Treasury

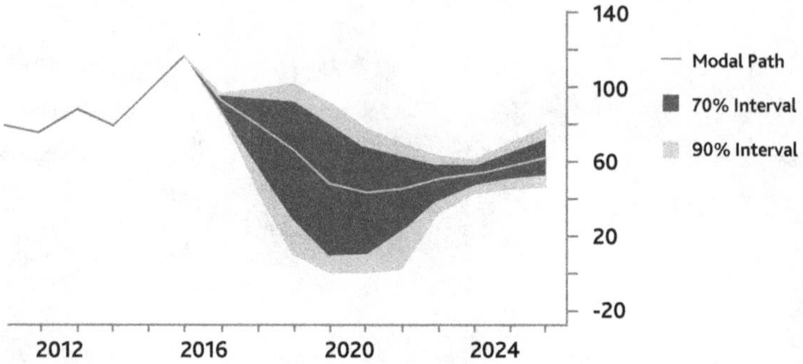

Source: Reproduced from Ferris et al. 2017.

Other Fiscal Consequences of a Floor System

To summarize: although the Fed's floor system is unlikely to render it insolvent anytime soon, the system is bound to have a higher fiscal cost than any sort of corridor system. That's because a floor system generally calls for a higher interest rate on *all* reserve balances, including balances that banks would hold even without the encouragement of interest on reserves. This in turn means a corresponding decline in Treasury remittances.

From a strictly utilitarian perspective, this increased fiscal cost is not necessarily a bad thing. For although it reduces the Fed's surplus, and with it the U.S. Treasury's revenue, that reduction in producer's surplus has as its counterpart an increase in consumers' surplus, consisting of increased commercial bank earnings, at least some of which are passed on to commercial bank depositors in the form of higher rates on commercial bank deposits. The Friedman rule is, after all, supposed to lead to precisely this outcome. However, for reasons discussed earlier, because a floor system generally involves interest payments in excess of those required to implement the Friedman rule, a corridor system with a below-market IOER rate is better suited for achieving an "optimum" return on reserve balances.

Furthermore, as David Beckworth (2017) has noted, such a strictly utilitarian perspective ignores "an important political-economy consideration," to wit: that the main recipients of interest on reserves are some foreign banks and the very largest U.S. banks. This, Beckworth observes, makes for some particularly "bad optics":

> Think about the implications: the banks that were bailed out during the crisis and the banks owned by foreigners are getting most of the IOER payment. This is a perfect storm of financial villains for both the political left and the right. . . . [T]he bad optics will only look worse if the Fed's balance sheet does not shrink as interest rates go up. For the IOER payment will go up too.

For this reason, as Cavallo et al. (2018, p. 14) also recognize, "large payments to the banking system could result in political pressure against maintaining or raising the IOER."[61]

But by far the most serious fiscal danger posed by a floor system stems from the fact that, under such a system, the size of the Fed's balance sheet ceases to have a crucial bearing upon the stance of monetary policy. Although—as I've noted above—the much-vaunted monetary control advantages of this "decoupling" of balance sheet policy from monetary policy are quite dubious, it has a very real political disadvantage, to which both Charles Plosser (2017) and I (Selgin 2017b) have drawn attention. As Plosser (2017, p. 6) explains, the fact that, under the floor system, the Fed's balance sheet can be made arbitrarily large "without

---

[61] For examples of these "bad optics" at work in popular publications, see Durden (2017) (*ZeroHedge*), "Is the Federal Reserve Giving Banks a $12bn Subsidy?" (2017) (*The Economist*), Richter (2018) (*Business Insider*), and Heller (2016) (*American Banker*). The last asks his readers to "Think of the potential political firestorms that will erupt as commercial banks are paid an amount equivalent to $100 billion per year that could otherwise be used to shore up federal resources."

impacting the conduct of monetary policy" (ibid., p.6), raises a crucial question, namely, "How and who will determine the amount of excess reserves created"? (ibid., p. 7):

> Making the Fed's balance sheet unrelated to monetary policy, opens the door for the Fed to use its balance sheet for other purposes. For example, the Fed would be free to engage in credit policy through the management of its assets while not impinging on monetary policy. Indeed, the Fed's balance sheet could serve as a huge intermediary and supplier of taxpayer subsidies to selected parties through credit allocation (ibid.).

Because it makes the size of the Fed's balance sheet "a free parameter" (ibid., p. 8), the new arrangement "also opens the door for Congress (or the Fed) to use the balance sheet for its own purposes (ibid., p. 7). "Congress," Plosser observes,

> would be free to lobby the Fed through political pressure or legislation to manage the portfolio for political ends. Imagine a Congress proposing a new infrastructure bill where the Fed was expected, or even required, to buy designated development bonds to support and fund the initiative so taxes could be deferred. This would be very tempting for Congress. Indeed, in testimony before Congress I was asked why the Fed shouldn't contribute "its fair share" to an infrastructure initiative. Imag[ine] the lobbying for the Fed to purchase "build America bonds" issued by the Treasury to fund infrastructure initiatives. . . . Of course, this just represents off-budget fiscal policy . . . Congress will undoubtedly find many "appropriate" uses for the Fed's balance sheet and could do so and claim it doesn't interfere with the independence of monetary policy" (ibid., p. 8).

One may also view the problem as one stemming from the fact that in a floor system, even very large Fed asset purchases no longer result in substantial changes in the price level. "Fear of inflation," I observed not long before Plosser's essay appeared, "has kept a lid on the Fed's financing of deficits" for decades. But in the new set-up, that constraint no longer operates:

> Now, if the Fed decides to gobble-up still more Treasury or government-agency securities, putting a like sum of fresh reserves at banks' disposal, it can still keep inflation at bay by hiking the IOER rate enough to bribe banks to hoard the reserves instead of lending them out (Selgin 2017b).

Nor can growth in the Fed's balance sheet itself be counted upon to provoke a public outcry:

> While inflation makes headlines, reserve hoarding doesn't. That's why the Brave New World of interest on reserves is so dangerous. Faced with the usual pressure to help the government pay its bills, Fed officials, and a pliant or weak Fed Chair especially, might cave-in to the government's demands while still meeting the Fed's inflation targets. In theory they could go on meeting the government's demands until every penny in bank deposits is financing some government spending, leaving nothing for private-sector borrowers.

Here, as in Plosser's argument, the concern is that because it "creates the opportunity and incentive for political actors to exploit the Fed's balance sheet to conduct off-budget fiscal policy and credit allocation," the Fed's floor system could "undermine Fed independence and politicize the Fed to a far greater degree than currently exists" (Plosser 2017, pp. 13–14). There is even reason to fear that by exploiting the Fed's floor system in pursuit of its own projects, Congress might ultimately cause the Fed to go broke after all, thereby dealing a further, and very severe, blow to its independence.

12

THE FLOOR SYSTEM AND POLICY NORMALIZATION

The Fed's Plan

Ever since the Fed began its large-scale asset purchases, Fed officials have been promising that once recovery from the crisis was complete, they would begin a process of monetary policy "normalization." In particular, they promised to eventually reduce the size of the Fed's balance sheet, though they announced a specific plan for doing so only in September 2014. They've also promised to get the Fed's policy rate settings back to "normal" levels.

Regarding the latter aim, most Fed officials now take for granted a long-run "normal" fed funds rate level of about 2.8 percent (lowered in 2017 from a 3 percent estimate), reflecting an assumed normal real rate—"r-star," in Fedspeak—of .8 percent, plus the Fed's 2 percent inflation target. Having the effective fed funds rate approach 2.8 percent is therefore also part of their normalization strategy. To judge by FOMC members' most recent (March 21, 2018) projections, as shown in Figure 12.1, that goal, or something close, will be reached within the next year or two, which is to say, while the Fed is still in the process of shrinking its balance sheet.

The Fed's plan for shrinking its balance sheet, which it unveiled in June 2014 and started to implement in October 2017, calls for it to shed $1.5 trillion in assets between now and 2022,

Figure 12.1: FOMC R-Star "Dot Plot," March 2018

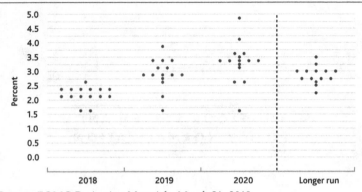

Source: FOMC Projection Materials, March 21, 2018.

bringing its balance sheet to $3 trillion, or to about 15 percent of projected 2022 GDP (Board of Governors 2017a). James Hamilton (2017) has illustrated the progress of the Fed's unwind in several nice charts, one of which is reproduced as Figure 12.2. Beside showing the slow pace of the Fed's unwind, the chart also shows that once the balance sheet declines to $3 trillion or so, it is expected to start swelling again.

Figure 12.2: Actual and Projected Federal Reserve Assets, 2002–2025

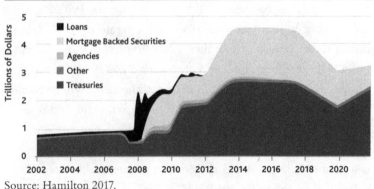

Source: Hamilton 2017.

The Fed's normalization plan has been criticized on several grounds. First, because the Fed's unwind allows for no outright asset sales, while placing varying limits or "caps" on the value of assets it will allow to roll off its balance sheet during any particular month, its pace is disappointingly languid.[62] Consequently, the Fed's credit footprint—and its influence on credit allocation—will also decline only very slowly. The Fed might easily have arranged to unwind at a faster yet still regular pace by combining higher roll-off caps with occasional active asset *sales* during low roll-off periods. According to Willem Buiter (2010), the impediments to a quick unwind are not technical but political. They consist of resistance from Treasury authorities seeking to avoid a sharp decline in the value of their securities as well as the Fed's own reluctance to draw attention to

> the true extent of the central bank's quasi-fiscal activities during the crisis and its aftermath. The large-scale ex-ante and ex-post quasi-fiscal subsidies handed out by the Fed and to a lesser extent by the other leading central banks, and the sheer magnitude of the redistribution of wealth and income among private agents that the central banks have engaged in could (and in my view should) cause a political storm. Delay in the dropping of the veil is therefore likely (ibid., p. 23).

Second, even at its minimum level, the Fed's balance sheet will be far larger, relative to the size of the U.S. economy, than it was prior to the crisis. Were the Fed intent on getting its balance sheet back on its precrisis trajectory by the end of 2020, it would be

---

[62] Having begun in October 2017 with maximum roll-offs of $6 billion in Treasuries and $4 billion in MBS, the Fed plans to increase the caps by those same amounts every three months for a year, after which they'll remain fixed at $30 billion for Treasury securities and $20 billion for MBS. Whenever the value of maturing assets of either sort exceeds its assigned cap, the Fed plans to reinvest the difference.

planning on slimming down by at least another $500 billion, and perhaps by another $1 trillion. As Ulrich Bindseil (2016, p. 227) explains, there are good reasons for wishing to see the Fed go on a more aggressive diet:

> While in crisis times, there are a number of justifications for lengthening the central bank balance sheet through LSAPS or LOLR [lender of last resort] operations . . . a lean balance sheet [in normal times] suggests that the central bank focuses on the core of its mandate. Moreover, a lean balance sheet is a sign of well-functioning financial markets and a healthy economy because the central bank is neither used as intermediary by the banking system, nor does the central bank see a need to engage in special crisis measures such as LSAPs.

"An outstandingly lean central bank balance sheet," Bindseil goes on to say, was among the Fed's principal merits before the crisis, when its total assets were "only around 1.1 times the total amount of bank notes in circulation" (ibid., p. 228).

Finally, the Fed's determination to raise its policy rate (or rates) to a preconceived "normal" level, and to do so within a relatively rapid span of time, seems imprudent, and may, if pursued obstinately, ultimately cause it to further delay its planned balance sheet reduction, or even to abandon it altogether.[63] The FOMC, Yellen said in her July 2017 testimony, was

> prepared to resume reinvestments if a material deterioration in the economic outlook were to warrant a sizable reduction in the federal funds rate. More generally, the committee would

---

[63] This was written in March 2018. Since then the *New York Times* ("Market Rate Rise May Thwart Fed's Balance Sheet Plan," June 27, 2018) has reported that the Fed's unwind has already led to some considerable, unanticipated tightening in the fed funds market, which tightening, should it continue, might "force the Federal Reserve to stop shrinking its balance sheet sooner than planned."

be prepared to use its full range of tools, including altering the size and composition of its balance sheet, if future economic conditions were to warrant a more accommodative monetary policy than can be achieved solely by reducing the federal funds rate (Yellen 2017b).[64]

A New Normal?

But to harp on these problems is to overlook the elephant in the room, to wit: the Fed's floor system and its desire to keep it.

Although the Fed never mentions that desire in laying out its normalization plan, its presence supplies a parsimonious explanation for several of that plan's details, and most obviously for the limited extent of the Fed's planned diet. Thus Hamilton (2017) argues, correctly, that as long as the Fed sticks to its present operating framework, the volume of reverse repos it conducts, as well as the value of Treasury balances held with it, will remain highly volatile, and that it will take "a lot of reserves sloshing around the system to cover that kind of variation." However, as Hamilton also notes, it would be easy enough for the Fed to make all that extra cash unnecessary if it wanted to, the most straightforward solution being that of "moving to a true corridor system for

---

[64] In fact, there is considerable disagreement, even within the Fed, concerning the likelihood that r-star (the equilibrium real federal funds rate) will reach 1 percent within the next several years. For example, in their recent San Francisco Fed study, Jens Christensen and Glenn Rudebusch (2017b) use Treasury Inflation-Protected Securities (TIPS) prices to arrive at what they consider to be especially reliable r-star estimates and projections. They conclude that as of December 2016, r-star stood close to zero, and that it "is more likely than not to remain near its current low for the foreseeable future" (ibid., p. 27). Elsewhere, the same authors (Christensen and Rudebusch 2017a) observe that, "For policymakers and researchers, the equilibrium interest rate provides a neutral benchmark to calibrate the stance of monetary policy: Monetary policy is expansionary if the short-term real interest rate lies below the equilibrium rate and contractionary if it lies above. Therefore, determining a good estimate of the equilibrium real rate has been at the center of recent policy debates."

controlling interest rates." Because a more abundant supply of bank reserves is a necessary feature of any floor-type operating system, the Fed's inclination to retain such a system may at least partly account for its desire to stay pudgy.[65]

The Fed's determination to stick to a floor system marks a major switch from its original understanding of what policy normalization entailed. Back in February 2010, when he first testified before Congress on what was then still referred to as the Fed's "exit strategy," Ben Bernanke (2010a) told Congress that the Fed "anticipates that it will eventually return to an operating framework with much lower reserve balances than at present and with the federal funds rate as the operating target for policy." In a footnote to his written testimony, Bernanke made it clear that he had a corridor system in mind:

> The authority to pay interest on reserves is likely to be an important component of the future operating framework for monetary policy. For example, one approach is for the Federal Reserve to bracket its target for the federal funds rate with the discount rate above and the interest rate on excess reserves below. Under this so-called corridor system, the ability of banks to borrow at the discount rate would tend to limit upward spikes in the federal funds rate, and the ability of banks to earn interest at the excess reserves rate would tend to contain downward movements (ibid., n9).

---

[65] Other arguments have, to be sure, been advanced for having the Fed retain a much-enlarged balance sheet. For these see Greenwood (2016) and Buiter, Jensen, and Rojas (2017). For an able reply, see Goodhart (2017). Among other points, Goodhart observes that while these authors "present arguments for not shrinking a Central Bank's [specifically, the Fed's] balance sheet from its present level, they advance none for further increasing it. Since the present level was largely attained by happenstance, proposals to maintain that (ad hoc) level suggest a lack of determining principles, and, perhaps a certain doubt" concerning the "strength of the underlying arguments."

Although Bernanke adds, in the same note, that "other approaches are also possible," and that the Fed "has ample time to consider the best long-run framework for policy implementation," the Fed was evidently inclined to return to an arrangement differing only modestly from its precrisis system. Apart from being reasonably consistent with a literal understanding of "normalization," that plan would have realized, as a floor system could not, Bernanke's hope that the Fed would eventually settle on an operating framework that would not "impose costs and distortions on the banking system."

That top Fed officials have since had a change of heart is evident not only from the details of the Fed's subsequently unveiled normalization plan, including a long-run balance sheet roughly three times larger, relative to GDP, than its precrisis counterpart, but also from some of those officials' recent statements. Thus, although Janet Yellen (2016, p. 10) had once suggested that after normalization, IOER would serve as a "contingency tool" of monetary control only, "because we may need to purchase assets during future recessions to supplement conventional interest rate reductions," less than a year later, she observed that

> our current system is working well and has some important advantages. In particular, it's simple and efficient to operate, does not require active management of the supply of reserves, and, most importantly, provides good control over the federal funds rate and effective transmission of changes in the federal funds rate to broader money market rates. And because our current system is likely compatible with the much smaller quantity of reserves, our plan for gradually reducing our balance sheet does not constrain the Committee's future options for how to implement monetary policy (Yellen 2017a, pp. 5–6).

Yellen also said that "changing the target *range* for the federal funds rate" would remain the Fed's "primary means of adjusting the stance of monetary policy" and that the Fed did not intend to treat the Fed's balance sheet as "an active tool for monetary policy in *normal* times" (my emphasis). Taking that last remark to rule out not just Quantitative Easing but also ordinary open-market operations as means for influencing the fed funds rate, Yellen's statement suggested that the Fed was by then inclined to stick to a floor system.

In a speech he gave two weeks earlier, at the Economic Club of New York (Powell 2017), then Governor Powell was forthright concerning his own preferences:

> [W]hen the [Federal Open Market] Committee discussed using a floor system as part of its longer-run framework, I was among those who saw such an approach as "likely to be relatively simple and efficient to administer, relatively straightforward to communicate, and effective in enabling interest rate control across a wide range of circumstances."
>
> Some have advocated a return to a framework similar to the pre-2007 system, in which the volume of reserves would likely be far below its present level and the federal funds rate would be managed by frequent open market operations. This "corridor" framework remains a feasible option, although, in my view, it may be less robust over time than a floor system.

More recently, retiring New York Fed President William Dudley (2018) and Vice-President Lorie Logan (2018) have both spoken in favor of retaining the Fed's floor system on the grounds that keeping it makes it unnecessary for the Fed to rely on routine open market operations to offset "autonomous" shocks to supply of or demand for bank reserves and also (according to Dudley) because it does away with the constraints on emergency lending implicit to a corridor system.

So, why not keep the floor system? First, because, as we've seen and despite what some Fed officials say, it hasn't worked all that well in practice. True, it has succeeded in keeping the effective fed funds rate within the Fed's "target range." But since the present system practically confines fed funds transactions to loans from GSEs to banks, where the GSEs have no reason to make the loans unless they can earn more than the Fed's ON-RRP rate, and banks have no reason to borrow from the GSEs unless they can do so for less than the IOER rate, such success is nugatory. A less trivial test of success is the extent to which the Fed's own policy rate changes have translated quickly into corresponding changes in other market interest rates, and with respect to this test, the success of the new arrangement is far less evident. Instead, several studies thus far have concluded that the switch from the Fed's traditional operating framework to its current IOER-based system of monetary control was marked by a less efficient overall "pass-through" of policy rate changes to market interest rates.[66]

Assessed in light of the Fed's ultimate policy goals, rather than as a mere means for altering interest rates, the Fed's new operating framework must be judged still more defective, in part because Fed officials originally employed it not to keep the Fed's policy rate at a level consistent with those goals but to hold it above that level. Because it put paid to the normal "multiplier" effect of open market purchases, the new framework also set the stage for still another dubious monetary policy experiment—the Fed's Large-Scale Asset Purchases—the real benefits of which remain controversial. That the combination of a floor system and LSAPs has dramatically increased the Fed's role in financial

---

[66] See Bech et al. (2014); Mora (2014); Duffie and Krishnamurthy (2016); Klee et al. (2016); and Kroeger and Sarket (2016). These findings are at least partly attributable to the change in the Fed's operating framework. To the extent that IOER rates exceed other money-market rates, Klee et al. (2016, p. 10) explain, banks lack any incentive to arbitrage the difference between rates in those markets and the effective fed funds rate.

intermediation by reducing bank lending to all kinds of other borrowers, especially by doing away with unsecured interbank lending, is on the other hand incontestable.

Corner versus Interior Solutions

In making the case for sticking with a floor system, Fed officials and economists (e.g., Lipscomb et al. 2017; Dudley 2018; and Logan 2018) observe that it "is operationally much less complex than a corridor system" (Dudley 2018) in that it reduces the need for routine open market operations to limit departures of the effective federal funds rate from its assigned target.[67] The argument is valid as far as it goes. But it fails to go far enough because it overlooks the *costs* that go hand-in-hand with the gains that Fed officials like to harp upon. As Ulrich Bindseil and Jukliusz Jablecki (2011) have compellingly argued, to arrive at a sound decision regarding a central bank's optimal operating framework, one has to take all relevant trade-offs—that is, all of the costs and benefits of alternative arrangements—into account.

One has to recognize, furthermore, that rather than facing a simple choice between a floor system on the one hand and a corridor system on the other, the Fed and other central banks face a much larger menu of options, including corridor systems of varying widths.[68] Other things being equal, a narrower corridor, by automatically limiting the variance of interbank

---

[67] This and the following paragraph draw on Selgin (2018b). Were the Fed's particular floor system not "leaky," the effective fed funds rate would be identical to the IOER rate, if only in the sense that there would be no actual trading of fed funds, hence no observed trades at non-IOER rates. As we've seen, in the system as it stands, some open market operations, consisting of ON-RRPs, are employed to limit the range of non-IOER trades.

[68] Concerning other "key dimensions" of corridor-system design, see Bindseil (2016, p. 17).

rates around their target, makes conducting monetary policy less "complex" than a broader one, though still more complicated than a floor system. Although it makes interest-rate targeting more challenging, a broad corridor is also conducive to having both a very active interbank market and a "lean" central bank balance sheet.

If there's to be a reasonable debate about the Fed's future operating system, participants in that debate need to recognize that within the broad set of available alternatives, a floor system represents an extreme, "corner" solution—one that can be likened to a zero-width corridor system.[69] Were it not for "leaks" in the Fed's floor, the solution, combined with an abundant supply of bank reserves, would keep the effective fed funds rate precisely on target at all times, without any need for Fed open market operations. However, it would do so only by reducing the volume of unsecured interbank lending to zero.

In a proper corridor system, on the other hand, as the corridor widens, both the variance of the effective funds rate around its targeted value and the volume of unsecured interbank lending increase, other things (including the frequency and scale of central bank open market operations) being equal. Figure 12.3, taken from Bindseil (2014, p. 79) and based on his and Jarecki's (2011) simulation study, illustrates these tendencies. Although the increased policy rate variance that goes along with a non-zero rate corridor (or, what amounts to the same thing, the additional

---

[69] In a true zero-width corridor system, the interest rate on reserves and the central bank's lending rate are both set equal to its policy rate. As Bindseil (2014, pp. 51–54) explains, a floor system, in which the interest rate on reserves only is set at the central bank's intended policy rate, and reserves are abundant, is one of two possible "one-directional" central bank operating frameworks. The other is an arrangement in which the central bank sets its standing-facility lending rate at its intended policy rate, while making sure that banks must always borrow from it to stay liquid.

Figure 12.3: Simulated Overnight Interbank Trading Volume (top) and Interest-Rate Volatility (bottom) for Different Corridor Widths and Money-Market Transaction Costs (C)

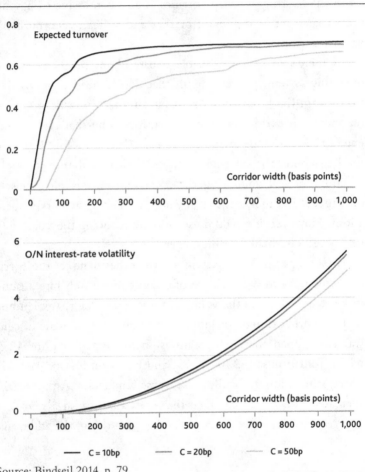

Source: Bindseil 2014, p. 79.

open market operations required to maintain a desired variance) may itself be reckoned a bad thing, the increased volume of inter-bank lending (and associated, smaller central bank credit foot-print) carries some offsetting benefits. The figure also shows that even a relatively narrow corridor of, say, 50 basis points, involving a modest increase in policy rate variance (or a correspondingly modest increase in offsetting central bank open market operations), may be all it takes to generate a substantial volume of interbank lending.[70]

Economists tend to be wary of corner solutions for the good reason that they're seldom optimal. Assuming that both the variance of the central bank target rate and the volume of interbank trades are each concave functions of the width of the rate corridor, as Bindseil and Jablecki (2011) determine to be the case by means of their simulation study, a floor system is unlikely to be an exception to the general rule. Instead, as Bindseil (2014, p. 80) concludes elsewhere,

> it seems plausible that a central bank with normally shaped preferences in [sic] both a stable overnight rate and a healthy market turnover will prefer an interior value for the width of the corridor, i.e., neither a very narrow nor an extremely wide corridor.

The general superiority of corridor systems, transition costs aside, and the challenge of unwinding those central bank balance sheets that grew substantially during the crisis and recession, helps to explain why the Fed, the Bank of England, and the ECB

---

[70] Apart from having a relatively narrow corridor, other aspects of corridor-system design can also reduce the need for open market operations to limit deviations of the overnight interbank rate from its target. For example, reserves "averaging"—meaning the practice of allowing banks' reserve holdings to occasionally fall short of required levels as long as the average level of those holdings over an extended maintenance period meets the requirement—can eliminate the need for open market interventions to stabilize the overnight rate except at the end of each maintenance period. The Bank of England successfully employed this approach between May 2006 and March 2009, when it switched to a floor system. For discussions of the relative merits of the Bank of England's pre- and post-March 2009 operating systems, see Winters (2012, pp. 35–44) and Clews et al. (2010).

alone still retain floor systems.[71] Other central banks that entered the crisis with corridor systems of some kind either (1) stuck to those systems all along (e.g., the Riksbank and the Reserve Bank of Australia); (2) switched to a floor system temporarily, and then reverted to a corridor (the Bank of Canada); or (3) switched first to floor systems and then to "tiered" or "quota" systems in which reserves can earn the policy rate only up to a certain limit, after which they earn lower, if not negative, rates (the Swiss National Bank, Bank of Japan, and Norges Bank). Finally, the only two central banks that relied on floor systems before the crisis began—Norges Bank and the Reserve Bank of New Zealand—also switched to tiered systems afterwards. They did so, moreover, to counter "banks' insatiable appetite for reserves" and thereby revive interbank lending (Sellin and Åsberg 2014; see also Berhardsen and Kloster 2010 and Akram and Findreng 2017).[72]

---

[71] According to Bill Nelson (2018), an officer in the Board of Governors' Division of Monetary Affairs between 2008 and 2016, it was only when the Fed's QE3 program went on for 15 months longer than originally planned—thereby more than doubling the Fed's total QE3 asset purchases—that Fed officials abandoned their original plan to eventually restore the Fed's precrisis operating system. Rather than being inspired by Fed officials' desire to "support efficient monetary policy," Nelson writes, the change was instead motivated by their unwillingness to have the Fed incur the capital losses that a more aggressive balance-sheet unwind would entail.

[72] Concerning New Zealand's experience, see Selgin (2018a). According to Norges Bank (2011), its switch from a floor to a quota system had two objectives. "One was to stop growth in central bank reserves. The other was to generate more interbank activity in the overnight market as rising quantities of reserves in the banking system entailed a risk that Norges Bank would assume some of the functions of the interbank market. The role of the central bank is to steer the total amount of reserves, while banks should redistribute the reserves overnight in the interbank market."

Bindseil (2016) undertakes a thorough assessment of alternative central bank operating frameworks, the conclusion of which is that "the symmetric corridor continues to perform well" relative to other alternatives.

That several countries have found it worthwhile to adopt tiered rather than corridor systems raises the question whether the Fed should consider that option as well. The disadvantage of a tiered system compared to a corridor consists of a still enlarged central bank credit footprint, albeit one that cannot be arbitrarily increased. The advantage is that a tiered system allows the Fed to endow the banking system with an extra cushion of liquid reserves, without raising minimum reserve requirements and without imposing any costs at all on banks.

In the United States today, however, it isn't clear what advantage any such enlarged liquidity cushion would serve beyond what can be had in a corridor system. After all, the modest IOER rate that a proper corridor system allows for will itself enhance banks' liquidity, mainly by discouraging them from using sweep accounts to avoid minimum reserve requirements. Current LCR requirements, furthermore, require that banks hold substantial quantities of high-quality liquid assets consisting either of reserves or of securities that can always serve as collateral for secured interbank loans. If modest IOER rates, minimum reserve requirements, and LCR rules are suspenders, an additional tier of zero opportunity cost excess reserves is a belt. One alone ought to do.

Though the claim may seem paradoxical, these arguments against a floor system don't mean that such a system is *never* warranted. In fact, it may be warranted, but only when there's no other choice: even the best-designed corridor system may temporarily function as de facto floor system under extreme circumstances, as when a surfeit of liquidity or declining natural rate or both drive the overnight rate to its corridor lower bound (the IOER rate), and especially when, for legal or technical reasons, that lower bound itself can't be lowered any further. But the occasional necessity of a floor system *in extremis* is no argument for an institutionalized floor system, particularly for a floor system with a positive IOER rate, which as we've seen amounts to a device for creating a liquidity trap when such a trap might not exist otherwise.

A Plan for Genuine Normalization

If the Fed's current normalization plan has been informed by Fed officials' desire to keep the present floor system in place, moving from that system to a corridor system, like the one Fed officials had in mind in 2006 (when they first gained permission to pay interest on bank reserves), calls for a different—and more ambitious—plan.

The present system rests on two requirements. First, it requires that excess reserves yield at least as much interest as money-market loans and low-risk, short-term securities. Second, it requires that supply of reserves (federal funds) be more than sufficient to equate quantity supplied and quantity demanded at the going IOER rate. A corridor system requires, on the other hand, that banks incur an opportunity cost by holding excess reserves, so that they're inclined to economize on reserves and make use of overnight interbank loans to meet occasional, short-term liquidity needs. The last condition guarantees that there will be an active federal funds market, with a market-clearing fed funds rate that can serve as an intermediate policy target, controllable by means of open market operations.

Moving from a floor system to a corridor is challenging because the move will entail an ultimately desirable revival of the once-moribund base money multiplier. As we've seen, for the M2 money stock, that multiplier is now less than half what it was before September 2008, so that reviving it could result in a doubling, or more, of the equilibrium money stock, nominal income, and the price level, other things being equal. To avoid missing its policy targets, the Fed would have to counter the multiplier's revival either by resorting to offsetting asset sales or by otherwise immobilizing excess reserves that banks are no longer inclined to hold. Given the huge quantity of excess reserves now outstanding, the Fed could find itself rushing to sell a corresponding amount of assets, upsetting markets. "No one," Karen Petrou (2016) has observed, "can forecast how still more trillions of assets set loose would fare, but it's clear that, at the very least, market volatility would spike, and financial stability would be endangered."

There's one obvious step the Fed can take to limit both the adverse effects of dealing adequately with a multiplier revival and the harm that would ensue from *not* dealing with it adequately. That consists of shrinking its balance sheet to the absolute minimum level required to maintain a floor system *before* it converts to a corridor system. While that shrinking is under way, the Fed could announce a new, temporary interest-rate target, based not on the effective funds rate (which is likely to behave especially erratically during the transition from a floor to a corridor system) but on one of the new Treasury repo reference rates unveiled by the Federal Reserve Bank in April 2018 (Federal Reserve Bank of New York 2018). Finally, once its balance sheet has reached the minimal level consistent with keeping banks flush with reserves, it can allow the IOER rate to fall below its new rate target, either passively (by leaving the IOER rate unchanged as the target rate rises) or, if necessary, by lowering the rate. Although the last step will trigger a revival of the money multiplier, which will in turn call for further open market sales to keep monetary policy on target, by shrinking its balance sheet in anticipation of this multiplier revival, the Fed will have minimized the quantity of such sales needed to prevent unwanted monetary expansion.

And the Fed might shrink its balance sheet, while still preserving its floor system, to a far greater extent than its present normalization plan would allow. In defense of the Fed's plan, Ben Bernanke (2017) observes that by December 2008, when the Fed's floor system was firmly established, "bank reserves were about $800 billion." "Taking into account growth in nominal GDP and bank liabilities," he added, suggests that "the critical level of bank reserves needed to implement monetary policy through a floor system seems likely to be well over $1 trillion today, and growing." However, the fact that banks held $800 billion in reserves in December 2008 doesn't at all imply that a smaller quantity of reserves would not have met the requirements of a floor system equally well. First, although it wasn't until December 2008 that the Fed officially switched from a single-value fed funds rate target to an IOER-based target range, the Fed was already operating a de-facto floor system by the end of October, when reserves were much lower. Second, as Stephen Williamson (2017a) points out, Canada's brief floor-system experience shows that although a floor system allows central banks to vastly expand the stock of bank reserves without significantly altering the stance of monetary policy, such a system doesn't require all that many more reserves than would suffice for a corridor system:

> How much [sic] reserves did it take to make [Canada's] floor system work? The Bank targeted overnight reserves to $3 billion (Canadian) over this period. To get an idea of the order of magnitude, a rule of thumb is that the Canadian economy is roughly a multiple of 10 of the US economy, so this quantity of reserves is roughly comparable to $30 billion in the US. We need to account for the fact that there are reserve requirements in the US, and none in Canada, and that the US institutional setup is very different (many more banks for example). But, I think it's hard to look at the Canadian experience and think that it takes as much as $1 trillion in interest bearing Fed liabilities to make a floor system work in the US, as Bernanke is suggesting. I would be surprised if we needed as much as $100 billion.

In other words, allowing for the demand for currency, the Fed might operate its floor system today with a balance sheet of less than $1.7 trillion dollars, and might do so in 2020 with a balance sheet of below $2 trillion, or over $1 trillion less than that provided for by its current normalization plan. Indeed, since that plan, in extrapolating from recent trends, may well overstate the future demand for currency, a 2020 balance sheet of considerably less than $2 trillion might suffice.[73] Nor are these estimates especially conservative. Ricardo Reis (2016, p. 463), for one, goes further, maintaining that "keeping the market for reserves saturated is consistent with returning to a *lean* central-bank balance sheet" (emphasis added). How lean? As of August 2016, Reis figured it would take a balance sheet of just $1 trillion, "or the size of the [Fed's] balance sheet in 2011." Allowing for the standard extrapolation, that would translate into a balance sheet of less than $1.3 trillion in 2020.

Nor need the Fed take much longer than until 2020 to achieve a substantially more aggressive unwind. As I've noted, its present plan, with its exclusive reliance upon capped roll-offs of maturing assets, is extremely conservative. By relaxing the roll-off caps while undertaking outright sales to compensate for low roll-off periods, the Fed could speed up its unwind considerably while still maintaining a smooth unwind schedule.

Until the Fed's balance sheet is reduced to the minimal level consistent with maintaining its floor system, the Fed should implement policy by adjusting its IOER and ON-RRP rates as needed to achieve its policy objectives, *not* merely according to some preconceived notion of a "normal" fed funds rate, as well as its announced schedule for arriving at it. But once the minimum reserve level is reached, it can proceed to the final steps toward genuine policy normalization. These steps are the most difficult

---

[73] As Hugh McCulloch observes (2018, p. 7), it is mainly owing to the persistence of very low interest rates that "currency in circulation has almost doubled since 2007, while the nominal economy has only grown about 33%," and that "this situation cannot be expected to continue forever."

because they must be carefully coordinated. One consists of a gradual *reduction* in the IOER rate aimed at raising the opportunity cost of holding excess reserves sufficiently to encourage banks that have been hoarding such reserves to dispose of them; the other consists of a further reduction in the nominal quantity of bank reserves, aimed at encouraging banks to routinely rely once again upon interbank borrowings to meet their liquidity needs. Ideally, because the one step reduces the demand for reserves while the other reduces their supply, the steps should be policy neutral.[74] However, they will ultimately change the way policy is implemented, by reviving the federal funds market, so that the Fed will be able to abandon its administered rate target "range" and once again target the effective fed funds rate.

During the transition itself, however, the Fed will need some way to both gauge and communicate its policy stance effectively. The challenge here is one Ben Bernanke (2010a, p. 10) addressed when he outlined the Fed's original "exit" strategy back in

---

[74] As Larry Wall (2017) observes, the balancing act won't necessarily be easy: "If the amount of sales ordered by the FOMC was too small, the resulting excessive stimulation would likely result in higher inflation. If the amount of sales was too large, the resulting excessive tightness could cause the economy to go into a recession." Wall is, of course, correct. But the problem he describes is one common to any scheme that relies upon balance sheet adjustments, routine or otherwise, to achieve a desired monetary policy stance during an episode of volatile reserve demand. There is some risk, on the other hand, that even starting with a minimized floor-system balance sheet, the asset sales needed to compensate for a sudden revival of wholesale bank lending might be large enough to disturb the markets for the assets being sold. Fortunately, the Fed has a ready-made solution to this problem in the shape of the Term Deposit Facility it established in early 2017 "to facilitate the conduct of monetary policy by providing a tool that may be used to manage the aggregate quantity of reserve balances held by depository institutions" (Central Bank Central 2017). The term deposit auctions undertaken by that facility serve, like Fed asset sales, to drain reserves from the banking system for the term of the auctioned deposits but do so without disrupting asset markets. The Fed might therefore rely upon such auctions, as it passes from a floor to a corridor regime, to achieve a steady further reduction of its balance sheet.

February 2010. To meet it, he said, the Fed might temporarily switch to "communicating the stance of policy in terms of another operating target, such as an alternative short-term interest rate." Fortunately, several very good alternatives are now available, consisting of benchmark rates developed recently by the Federal Reserve Bank of New York, based on private Treasury-secured overnight repos (Federal Reserve Bank of New York 2017).

Once the federal funds market is functioning as it did before the crisis, with substantial volumes of interbank lending and borrowing, the Fed can return to its traditional reliance upon open market operations to keep the effective federal funds rate at its chosen target level. Allowing that the Fed still pays interest on bank reserves, albeit at a rate that remains below the policy target rate, the new arrangement will differ only slightly from the Fed's pre-October 2008 system: instead of resembling the Fed's precrisis system, the new system will be a more orthodox corridor system of the sort Fed officials had in mind in 2006, when they were first granted permission to pay interest on bank reserves.

A Nudge from Congress

Achieving a genuine normalization of monetary policy, including a nondisruptive return to a corridor-type operating system, is, I've tried to suggest, difficult but perfectly possible. And even if it would be considerably more difficult than the Fed's present plan, which would keep the floor system in place indefinitely, that greater difficulty would not be a good reason for sticking to the current plan. As I've tried to show in some detail in these pages, the Fed's floor system of monetary control is both unreliable and inefficient. Because it severs the link between reserve creation and monetary expansion, it makes achieving monetary stimulus, even by means of extraordinary asset purchases, extremely difficult; and because it has the Fed borrowing heavily from private intermediaries, it replaces private-sector lending with lending to the U.S. Treasury and other government agencies. Finally, the Fed's floor system is inconsistent with the intent of the 2006 law that first granted the Fed the right to pay interest on bank reserves.

Ideally, Fed officials can still be convinced, in light of the floor system's serious shortcomings, to alter their plans and eventually switch to an orthodox corridor system. But whether they can or can't, Congress should make the Fed abide by the spirit of the 2006 law allowing the Fed to pay interest on reserves, either by clarifying that law's stipulation that rates paid on reserves not "exceed the general level of short-term interest rates,"[75] or by limiting interest payments to banks' required reserve balances only while allowing the Fed a period of no more than two years to comply with the revised statute. Should Fed officials still wish to have a floor system, they can always seek Congress's permission by proposing new legislation specifically granting them the necessary powers, which they've exercised thus far only by flouting the law. That, after all, is how democratic government is supposed to work.

---

[75] Appendix 2 suggests how the 2006 law might be amended to achieve this end.

Appendix 1

BANK LENDING AND THE INTEREST RATE ON EXCESS RESERVES

The argument in Chapter 8 that the Fed's positive IOER rate can cause a bank to lend less even when the IOER rate is substantially less than the bank's net interest margin agrees with the implications of many standard models of bank optimization. I offer here an example using a simplified version of Timothy Hannan's (1991) model, which is itself based on Michael Klein's (1971) "A Theory of the Banking Firm." My model differs from Hannan's in allowing for only one category of deposits instead of several, and in assigning to reserves the part that securities play in Hannan's model. The last change reflects the fact that the Fed's IOER rate has generally exceeded comparable rates on relatively safe, short-term securities, so that reserves strictly dominate securities in risk-adjusted return.

A representative bank maximizes its profit on an asset portfolio consisting of reserves (R) and N kinds of loans (L), differing in their riskiness and maturity, among other factors, financed by deposits (D):

$$\pi = \sum_{n}^{N} (r_L^n - C_L^n) \, L_n + r_R R - (r_D + c_D)D,$$

where r_L^n is the interest rate on loans of type n, and r_R and r_D are the interest rates paid on reserves and deposits, respectively. C_L^n is the noninterest expense, including loan-loss provisions, associated with a loan of type n, and c_D is the noninterest expense associated with maintaining and servicing deposits.

Banks maximize profit subject to the balance sheet constraint,

$$\sum_n^N (L_n) + R = D + K,$$

where K stands for bank capital. The first order condition for profit maximization is

$$\frac{\partial \pi}{\partial r_L^n} = L_n + r_L^n \frac{L_n}{dr_L^n} - (r_R + c_L^n) \frac{dL_n}{dr_L^n} = 0.$$

Defining the elasticity of demand for a type n loan as

$$e_L^n = -\left(\frac{r_L^n}{L_n}\right)\left(\frac{dL_n}{dr_L^n}\right) > 0,$$

that condition can be rewritten as

$$r_L^n = (r_R + c_L^n)\left[\frac{e_L^n}{e_L^n - 1}\right],$$

which shows that the bank's lending rate will increase as either the IOER rate or the noninterest costs of lending increases and will decline as the elasticity of loan demand increases. To paraphrase Hannan (p. 71), "The optimal loan rate is determined by the extent to which it is profitable to replace [reserves] with loans in the bank's portfolio." In other words, a higher IOER rate raises loan rates by causing banks to hoard cash instead of lending it.

As long as loan demand is elastic, the equilibrium loan rate will exceed the IOER rate. In the limit, as elasticity approaches infinity (as it does in the case of a banking industry that's either perfectly competitive or perfectly contestable), equilibrium lending rates will exceed the IOER rate by the noninterest cost of lending:

$$r_L^n = r_R + c_L^n.$$

Note that, if the noninterest expense associated with *any* loan type is zero, then the interest rate charged on those loans will equal the IOER rate. This case is like the one illustrated in Figure 8.5, where the marginal loan rate is assumed to be equal to the IOER rate. Product differentiation, to the extent that it exists, will widen the gap between equilibrium loan rates and the IOER rate still further.

Finally, let's consider what all this implies concerning the relation between net interest margins and the IOER rate. For the perfectly competitive (or contestable) market case, the net interest margin (NIM) for a loan of type n is

$$NIM_n = r_L^n - r_D = r_R + C_L^n - r_D.$$

The net interest margin for a type n loan will therefore exceed the IOER rate by the difference between the noninterest and interest expenses associated with the loan. In recent years, with deposit rates at extremely low levels, if not at zero, that difference has been substantial.

Since a bank's net loan income is equal to its net interest margin minus the noninterest expense of lending, including loan loss provisions, the equilibrium condition can be restated to be that a bank's marginal net loan income, expressed as an annual percentage, will tend to be equal to the difference between the IOER rate and the interest rate on deposits.

Appendix 2

PROPOSED AMENDMENT TO THE 2006 FINANCIAL SERVICES REGULATORY RELIEF ACT

As written, the 2006 Financial Services Regulatory Relief Act allows the Federal Reserve to pay interest on reserves "at a rate or rates not to exceed the general level of short-term interest rates" (12 U.S.C. 461 (b)(12)(A)). However, in drafting the final rules implementing the statute, as amended by the 2008 Emergency Economic Stabilization Act (which altered the timing of the 2006 act's provision only), Fed officials determined that for that purpose "'short-term interest rates' are rates on obligations with maturities of no more than one year, such as the primary credit rate and rates on term federal funds, term repurchase agreements, commercial paper, term Eurodollar deposits, and other similar instruments ("Regulation D: Reserve Requirements for Depository Institutions," *Federal Registrar*, June 22, 2015, p. 35567)." Because the Fed's primary credit rate is a rate it administers, rather than a market-determined rate, and because that rate is always set above the interest rate paid on bank reserves, the Fed's understanding of the meaning of "general level of short-term interest rates" allows *any* interest rate it chooses to pay on reserves to satisfy the statute's requirement!

To ensure that the Federal Reserve abides by the spirit of the 2006 law, the meaning of the phrase "general level of short-term interest rates" must be clarified. The interest rates that are most suitable for that purpose are market-determined rates on instruments similar in duration and risk to the reserve balances on which the Fed is authorized to pay interest. Because reserve balances are essentially very-low-risk assets of zero maturity, interest rates on private overnight repurchase agreements collateralized by Treasury securities are close market-determined equivalents.

Although there is no one uniform overnight repo rate, the Federal Reserve Bank of New York has recently conducted extensive research aimed at establishing overnight repo benchmark rates using transaction level data. Based on this research, the New York Fed has developed a "Broad Treasury financing rate" that's perfectly suited to serve as an IOR benchmark rate, that is, as a reference "general" rate for the purpose of implementing the statute.[76] In light of this, Congress should amend the 2006 Act by having "the general level of short-term interest rates" refer specifically to some value or values of the "Broad Treasury financing rate." For example, the text of the necessary amendment might read as follows:

Section 19(b)(12) of the Federal Reserve Act (12 U.S.C. 461(b)(12)) is amended by inserting after Subparagraph (C)

"(D) General level of short-term interest rates defined.

For purposes of this paragraph, the term 'general level of short-term interest rates' shall be defined as the average value over the preceding six-week interval of the Federal Reserve Bank of New York's benchmark Broad Treasury financing rate on overnight repurchase agreements."

---

[76] For details, see Bayeux et al. (2017) and Federal Reserve Bank of New York (2017).

REFERENCES

Afonso, Gara, Alex Entz, and Eric LeSueur. 2013. "Who's Lending in the Fed Funds Market?" *Liberty Street Economics*, Federal Reserve Bank of New York, December 2. http://libertystreeteconomics .newyorkfed.org/2013/12/whos-lending-in-the-fed-funds-market .html

Afonso, Gara, Anna Kovner, and Antoinette Schoar. 2011. "Stressed, Not Frozen: The Fed Funds Market in the Financial Crisis." *Journal of Finance* 66 (4) (August): 1109–39.

Akram, Q. Farooq, and Jon H. Findreng. 2017. "Norwegian Interbank Market's Response to Changes in Liquidity Policy." Norges Bank Working Paper 7/2017, April 20. https://static.norges-bank.no/ contentassets/80a539f28a1d46c5b1dba6ce5e2ef55f/working _paper_7_17.pdf

Alper, Koray, Mahir Binici, Selva Demiralp, Hakan Kara, and Pınar Ozlu. 2016. "Reserve Requirements, Liquidity Risk, and Bank Lending Behavior," Koç University-TUSIAD Economic Research Forum Working Papers 1612, Koc University-TUSIAD Economic Research Forum, November. https://ideas.repec.org/p/koc/wpaper /1612.html#download

Amal, Dean F., and Timothy H. Hannan. 1999. "Establishing Banking Market Definitions through Estimations of Residual Deposit Supply Equations." *Journal of Banking and Finance* 23 (11) (February): 1667–90. https://www.sciencedirect.com/science/article/pii/S037842669 9000187

Andolfatto, David. 2015. "A Model of U.S. Monetary Policy Before and After the Great Recession." Federal Reserve Bank of St. Louis *Review* 97 (3): 233–56. https://research.stlouisfed.org/publications/review/2015/09/08/a-model-of-u-s-monetary-policy-before-and-after-the-great-recession

Antinolfi, Gaetano, and Todd Keister. 2012. "Interest on Excess Reserves and Cash 'Parked' at the Fed." *Liberty Street Economics*, Federal Reserve Bank of New York, August 22. http://libertystreeteconomics.newyorkfed.org/2012/08/interest-on-excess-reserves-and-cash-parked-at-the-fed.html

Appelbaum, Binyamin. 2013. "A Bold Dissenter at the Fed, Hoping His Doubts Are Wrong." *New York Times*, January 8. http://www.nytimes.com/2013/01/09/business/a-bold-dissenter-at-the-fed-hoping-his-doubts-are-wrong.html

Arias, Maria A., and Yi Wen. 2014. "The Liquidity Trap: An Alternative Explanation for Today's Low Inflation." *Regional Economist*, April: 10–11. https://www.stlouisfed.org/publications/regional-economist/april-2014/the-liquidity-trap-an-alternative-explanation-for-todays-low-inflation

Asness, Cliff, et al. 2010. "Open Letter to Ben Bernanke." *Wall Street Journal*, November 15. https://blogs.wsj.com/economics/2010/11/15/open-letter-to-ben-bernanke/

Balatti, Mirco, Chris Brooks, Michael T. Clements, and Konstantina Kappou. 2016. "Did Quantitative Easing Only Inflate Stock Prices? Macroeconomic Evidence from the US and UK." Unpublished manuscript, September. https://papers.ssrn.com/sol3/papers.cfm?abstract_id=2838128

Ball, Laurence, Joseph Gagnon, Patrick Honohan, and Signe Krogstrup. 2016. "What Else Can Central Banks Do?" Geneva Reports on the World Economy, No. 18. https://cepr.org/sites/default/files/geneva_reports/GenevaP285.pdf

Banegas, Ayelen, and Manjola Tase. 2017. "Reserve Balances, the Federal Funds Market, and Arbitrage in the New Regulatory Framework." Unpublished working paper, September 13. https://papers.ssrn.com/sol3/papers.cfm?abstract_id=3055299

Bank of Canada. 2010. "Bank of Canada Increases Overnight Rate Target to ½ Per Cent and Re-establishes Normal Functioning of the Overnight Market." Press release, June 1. https://www.bankofcanada.ca/2010/06/fad-press-release-2010-06-01/

Barajas, Adolfo, Ralph Chami, Thomas Cosimano, and Dalia Hakura. 2010. "U.S. Bank Behavior in the Wake of the 2007-2009 Financial Crisis." IMF Working Paper WP/10/131, May. https://www.imf.org/en/Publications/WP/Issues/2016/12/31/U-S-23907

Barro, Robert J. 2016. "The Job-Filled Non-Recovery." Unpublished manuscript, Harvard University, September. https://www.brookings.edu/wp-content/uploads/2016/08/barro-remarks.pdf

Bassetto, Marco, and Todd Messer. 2013. "Fiscal Consequences of Paying Interest on Reserves." *Fiscal Studies* 34 (4): 413–36. http://onlinelibrary.wiley.com/doi/10.1111/j.1475-5890.2013.12014.x/abstract

Bayeux, Kathryn, Alyssa Cambron, Marco Cipriani, Adam Copeland, Scott Sherman, and Brett Solimine. 2017. "Introducing the Revised Broad Treasuries Financing Rate." *Liberty Street Economics*, Federal Reserve Bank of New York, June 19. http://libertystreeteconomics.newyorkfed.org/2017/06/introducing-the-revised-broad-treasuries-financing-rate.html

Bech, Morten L, Carl T. Bergstrom, Martin Rosvall, and Rodney J. Garratt. 2015. "Mapping Changes in the Overnight Money Market." *Physica A* **424**: 44–51. https://www.sciencedirect.com/science/article/pii/S0378437114009856

Bech, Morten L., Elizabeth Klee, and Viktors Stebunovs. 2014. "Arbitrage, Liquidity and Exit: The Repo and Federal Funds Markets Before, During, and Emerging from the Financial Crisis." In Jagjit S. Chadha, Alain C. J. Durré, Michael A. S. Joyce, and Lucio Sarno, *Developments in Macro-Finance Yield Curve Modelling*. Cambridge, UK: Cambridge University Press, pp. 293–325.

Beckworth, David. 2008. "Repeating the Fed's Policy Mistake of 1936–1937." *Macro Musings Blog*, October 29. http://macromarketmusings.blogspot.com/2008/10/repeating-feds-policy-mistake-of-1936.html

———. 2009. "What Was the Stance of Monetary Policy Late Last Year?" *Macro Musings Blog*, October 2. http://macromarketmusings.blogspot.com/2009/10/what-was-stance-of-monetary-policy-late.html

———. 2017. "Bad Optics: The Fed's Balance Sheet Edition." *Macro Musings Blog*, May 19. http://macromarketmusings.blogspot.com/2017/05/bad-optics-feds-balance-sheet-edition.html

_____. 2018. "The Great Divorce: The Fed's Move to a Floor System and its Implications for Bank Portfolios." Unpublished manuscript, January 31.

Belke, Angar, Daniel Gross, and Thomas Osowski. 2017. "The Effectiveness of the Fed's Quantitative Easing Policy: New Evidence Based on International Interest Rate Differentials." *Journal of International Money and Finance* 73: 335–49. https://www.sciencedirect.com/science/article/pii/S0261560617300293

Berentsen, Aleksander, Alessandro Marchesiani, and Christopher J. Waller. 2014. "Floor Systems for Implementing Monetary Policy: Some Unpleasant Fiscal Arithmetic. *Review of Economic Dynamics* 17 (3) (July): 532–42. https://www.sciencedirect.com/science/article/pii/S1094202513000471

Bernanke, Ben. 2009. "The Crisis and the Policy Response." Stamp Lecture, London School of Economics, London, England, January 13. https://www.federalreserve.gov/newsevents/speech/bernanke20090113a.htm

_____. 2010a. "Federal Reserve's Exit Strategy." Testimony before the Committee on Financial Services, U.S. House of Representatives, February 10. https://www.federalreserve.gov/newsevents/testimony/bernanke20100224a.pdf

_____. 2010b. "The Economic Outlook and Monetary Policy." Speech at the Federal Reserve Bank of Kansas City Economic Symposium, Jackson Hole, Wyoming, August 27. https://www.federalreserve.gov/newsevents/speech/bernanke20100827a.htm

_____. 2012. "Monetary Policy since the Onset of the Crisis." Speech at the Federal Reserve Bank of Kansas City Economic Symposium, Jackson Hole, Wyoming, August 31. https://www.federalreserve.gov/newsevents/speech/bernanke20120831a.htm

_____. 2015. *The Courage to Act.* New York: W.W. Norton.

_____. 2017. "Shrinking the Fed's Balance Sheet." *Ben Bernanke's Blog*, Brookings Institution, January 26. https://www.brookings.edu/blog/ben-bernanke/2017/01/26/shrinking-the-feds-balance-sheet/

Bernanke, Ben, and Donald Kohn. 2016. "The Fed's Interest Payments to Banks." *Ben Bernanke's Blog*, Brookings Institution, February 16. https://www.brookings.edu/blog/ben-bernanke/2016/02/16/the-feds-interest-payments-to-banks/

Bernhardsen, Tom, and Arne Kloster. 2010. "Liquidity Management System: Floor or Corridor?" Norges Bank Staff Memo No. 4. https://static.norges-bank.no/globalassets/upload/publikasjoner/staff-memo/2010/staff_memo_042010.pdf?v=03/09/2017122442&ft=.pdf

Berrospide, Jose, and Rochelle Edge. 2010. "The Effects of Bank Capital on Lending: What Do We Know, and What Does It Mean?" Federal Reserve Board of Governors Finance and Economics Discussion Series Paper No. 44: 1–48. https://www.federalreserve.gov/pubs/feds/2010/201044/201044pap.pdf

Bewley, Truman. 1980. "The Optimum Quantity of Money." In John Kareken and Neil Wallace, eds., *Models of Monetary Economics*. Minneapolis, Minnesota: Federal Reserve Bank of Minneapolis.

Bhattarai, Saroj, and Christopher Neely. 2016. "A Survey of the Empirical Literature on U.S. Unconventional Monetary Policy." Federal Reserve Bank of St. Louis Working Paper 2016-021A, October. https://files.stlouisfed.org/files/htdocs/wp/2016/2016-021.pdf

Bindseil, Ulrich. 2014. *Monetary Policy Operations and the Financial System*. Oxford: Oxford University Press.

_____. 2016. "Evaluating Monetary Policy Operational Frameworks." In *Designing Resilient Monetary Policy Frameworks for the Future*. Kansas City: Federal Reserve Bank of Kansas City, pp. 179–277. https://www.kansascityfed.org/~/media/files/publicat/sympos/2016/2016bindseil.pdf?la=en

Bindseil, Ulrich, and Juliusz Jabłecki. 2011. "The Optimal Width of the Central Bank Standing Facilities Corridor and Banks' Day-to-Day Liquidity Management." European Central Bank Working Paper Series No. 1350, June. https://www.ecb.europa.eu/pub/pdf/scpwps/ecbwp1350.pdf?c57bbfd0b940fd5fca75b653f1216120

Blasques, Francisco, Falk Bräuning, and Iman van Lelyveld. 2016. "A Dynamic Network Model of the Unsecured Interbank Lending Market." Federal Reserve Bank of Boston Working Paper No. 16-3, April. https://www.bostonfed.org/-/media/Documents/Workingpapers/PDF/wp1603.pdf

Blinder, Alan. 2012. "How Bernanke Can Get Banks Lending Again." *Wall Street Journal*, July 22. https://www.wsj.com/articles/SB10000872396390444873204577537212738938798

Board of Governors of the Federal Reserve System. 1971. "Record of Policy Actions of the FOMC." *Federal Reserve Bulletin* 12 (57) (December): 989–99. https://fraser.stlouisfed.org/scribd/?item_id=21440&filepath=/files/docs/publications/FRB/1970s/frb_081971.pdf

—————. 2002. "Alternative Instruments for Open Market and Discount Window Operations." Federal Reserve System Study Group on Alternative Instruments for System Operations. December. https://www.federalreserve.gov/boarddocs/surveys/soma/alt_instrmnts.pdf

—————. 2008a. "Conference Call of the Federal Open Market Committee." September 29. https://www.federalreserve.gov/monetarypolicy/files/FOMC20080929confcall.pdf

—————. 2008b. "Board Announces That It Will Begin to Pay Interest on Depository Institutions' Required and Excess Reserve Balances." Press Release, October 6. https://www.federalreserve.gov/newsevents/pressreleases/monetary20081006a.htm

—————. 2008c. "Transcript of the Federal Open Market Committee Meeting," December 15–16. https://www.federalreserve.gov/monetarypolicy/files/FOMC20081216meeting.pdf

—————. 2011. "Transcript of the Federal Open Market Committee," August 9. https://www.federalreserve.gov/monetarypolicy/files/FOMC20110809meeting.pdf

—————. 2012a. "Federal Reserve Issues FOMC Statement of Longer-Run Goals and Policy Strategy." Press Release, January 25. https://www.federalreserve.gov/newsevents/pressreleases/monetary20120125c.htm

—————. 2012b. "Transcript of the Federal Open Market Committee Meeting," July 3–August 1. https://www.federalreserve.gov/monetarypolicy/files/FOMC20120801meeting.pdf

—————. 2014. "Policy Normalization Principles and Plans." September 16. https://www.federalreserve.gov/monetarypolicy/files/FOMC_PolicyNormalization.pdf

—————. 2015. "Transcript of the Federal Open Market Committee Meeting," July 28–29. https://www.federalreserve.gov/monetarypolicy/files/fomcminutes20150729.pdf

—————. 2017a. "Policy Normalization." https://www.federalreserve.gov/monetarypolicy/policy-normalization.htm

_____. 2017b. "Policy Tools: The Discount Rate." https://www
.federalreserve.gov/monetarypolicy/discountrate.htm

_____. 2018. "FOMC Projection Materials." March 21.
https://www.federalreserve.gov/monetarypolicy/files/monetary
20180321a1.pdf

Borio, Claudio, and Piti Disyatat. 2009. "Unconventional Monetary
Policies: An Appraisal." BIS Working Paper No. 292. https://www
.bis.org/publ/work292.htm

Borio, Claudio, and Philip Lowe. 2002. "Asset Prices, Financial and
Monetary Stability: Exploring the Nexus." BIS Working Paper
No. 114. https://www.bis.org/publ/work114.htm

Bowman, David, Fang Cai, Sally Davies, and Steven Kamin. 2011.
"Quantitative Easing and Bank Lending: Evidence from Japan."
Federal Reserve Board of Governors International Finance
Discussion Paper No. 1018. https://www.federalreserve.gov/pubs/
ifdp/2011/1018/ifdp1018.pdf

Bowman, David, Etienne Gagnon, and Mike Leahy. 2010. "Interest on
Excess Reserves as a Monetary Policy Instrument: The Experience
of Foreign Central Banks." Federal Reserve Board of Governors
International Finance Discussion Paper No. 996: 1–47. https://www
.federalreserve.gov/pubs/ifdp/2010/996/ifdp996.pdf

Buiter, Willem H. 2010. "Reversing Unconventional Monetary Policy:
Technical and Political Considerations." In Morten Balling, Jan
Marc Berk, and Marc-Olivier Strauss-Kahn, eds., *The Quest for
Stability: The Macro View*. Vienna: SUERF, pp. 23–43. https://www
.suerf.org/docx/s_36e729ec173b94133d8fa552e4029f8b_2585_
suerf.pdf

Buiter, Willem H., Ebrahim Rahbari, Kim D. Jensen, and Cesar Rojas.
2017. "Why Does the Fed (or any Central Bank) Want to Shrink Its
Balance Sheet?" Citi Research, Global Economic Views 9, August.

Canzoneri, Matthew, Robert Cumby, and Behzad Diba. 2016. "Should
the Federal Reserve Pay Competitive Interest on Reserves?"
Unpublished manuscript, July 20. http://faculty.georgetown.edu/
cumbyr/papers/Optimal%20Interest%20on%20Reserves.pdf

Carpenter, Seth B., Jane E. Ihrig, Elizabeth C. Klee, Daniel W. Quinn,
and Alexander H. Boote. 2013. "The Federal Reserve's Balance Sheet
and Earnings: A Primer and Projections." Federal Reserve Board
Finance and Economics Discussion Series, Divisions of Research &

Statistics and Monetary Affairs, September. https://www.federal
reserve.gov/pubs/feds/2013/201301/revision/201301pap.pdf

Cavallo, Michelle, Marco Del Negro, W. Scott Frame, Jamie Grasing,
Benjamin A. Malin, and Carlo Rosa. 2018. "Fiscal Implications of
the Federal Reserve's Balance Sheet Normalization." Federal Reserve
Bank of New York Staff Report No. 833, January. https://www
.newyorkfed.org/medialibrary/media/research/staff_reports/sr833.pdf

Central Bank Central. 2017. "Term Deposit Facility Overview."
https://www.frbservices.org/assets/central-bank/tdf-overview.pdf

Chattopadhyay, Siddhartha, and Betty C. Daniel. 2017. "Taylor-Rule
Exit Policies for the Zero Lower Bound." Unpublished manuscript,
June 20. https://www.albany.edu/~bd892/Papers/TaylorRule.pdf

Chen, Han, Vasco Cúrdia, and Andrea Ferrero. 2012. "The Macroeconomic Effects of Large-Scale Asset Purchase Programs." Economic
Journal 122 (564) (November): F289–F315. http://www.jstor.org
.proxy-remote.galib.uga.edu/stable/23324225

Choulet, Céline. 2015. "QE and Bank Balance Sheets: the American
Experience." Conjuncture, July-August: 3–19. http://economic
-research.bnpparibas.com/pdf/en-US/QE-bank-balance-sheets
-American-experience-7/23/2015,25852

Christensen, Jens H. E., and Glenn D. Rudebusch. 2017a. "New Evidence
for a Lower New Normal in Interest Rates." Federal Reserve Bank
of San Francisco Economic Letter 2017-17, June 19. https://www.frbsf
.org/economic-research/publications/economic-letter/2017/june/
financial-market-evidence-for-lower-natural-interest-rate-r-star/

_____. 2017b. "A New Normal for Interest Rates? Evidence
from Inflation-Indexed Debt." Federal Reserve Bank of San
Francisco Working Paper 2017-07, May. https://www.frbsf.org
/economic-research/publications/working-papers/2017/07/

Clews, Roger, Chris Salmon, and Olaf Weeken. 2010. "The Bank's
Money Market Framework." Bank of England Quarterly Bulletin
Q4: 292–300. https://papers.ssrn.com/sol3/Delivery.cfm/SSRN
_ID1730151_code459244.pdf?abstractid=1730151&mirid=1&
type=2

Cohen, Patricia, and Jim Tankersley. 2018. "E-Commerce Might
Help Solve the Mystery of Low Inflation." New York Times, June 11.
https://www.nytimes.com/2018/06/11/business/economy/inflation
-internet.html

Constâncio, Vítor. 2016. "The Challenge of Low Real Interest Rates for Monetary Policy." Lecture at the Macroeconomics Symposium at Utrecht School of Economics, June 15. https://www.ecb.europa.eu/press/key/date/2016/html/sp160615.en.html

Cooper, Jonathan. 2012. "Fed's LSE Blog Chimes In on Why Not to Lower Interest on Excess Reserves Rate; We Think They Miss the Point." *Finadium* blog, August 28. http://finadium.com/feds-liberty-street-economics-blog-chimes-in-on-lowering-interest-on-excess-reserves-rate-much-ado-about-nothing/

Covas, Francisco B., Marcelo Rezende, and Cindy M. Vojtech. 2015. "Why are Net Interest Margins of Large Banks So Compressed?" *FEDS Notes*, October 5. https://www.federalreserve.gov/econresdata/notes/feds-notes/2015/why-are-net-interest-margins-of-large-banks-so-compressed-20151005.html

Craig, Ben, Sara Millington, and John Zito. 2014. "Who Is Holding All the Excess Reserves?" Federal Reserve Bank of Cleveland *Economic Trends* Report. https://www.clevelandfed.org/newsroom-and-events/publications/economic-trends/2015-economic-trends/et-20150811-who-is-holding-all-the-excess-reserves.aspx

De Gregorio, Jose, and Pablo E. Guidotti. 1995. "Financial Development and Economic Growth." *World Development* 23 (3), March: 433–48. https://www.sciencedirect.com/science/article/pii/0305750X9400132I

Del Negro, Marco, and Christopher A. Sims. 2015. "When Does a Central Bank's Balance Sheet Require Fiscal Support?" *Journal of Monetary Economics* 73 (July): 1–19. https://www.sciencedirect.com/science/article/pii/S0304393215000604

Dell'Ariccia, Giovanni, Vikrim Haksar, and Tommaso Mancini-Griffoli. 2017. "Negative Interest Rate Policies—Initial Experiences and Assessments." IMF Policy Paper, August. https://www.imf.org/en/Publications/Policy-Papers/Issues/2017/08/03/pp080317-negative-interest-rate-policies-initial-experiences-and-assessments

Demiralp, S., J. Eisenschmidt, and T. Vlassopoulos. 2017. "Negative Interest Rates, Excess Liquidity, and Bank Business Models: Banks' Reaction to Unconventional Monetary Policy in the Euro Area." Unpublished working paper. May. https://papers.ssrn.com/sol3/Delivery.cfm/SSRN_ID2972481_code185187.pdf?abstractid=2941377&mirid=1

Duarte, Fernando, and Anna Zabai. 2015. "An Interest Rate Rule to Uniquely Implement the Optimal Equilibrium in a Liquidity Trap." Federal Reserve Bank of New York Staff Report No. 745, October. https://www.newyorkfed.org/medialibrary/media/research/staff_reports/sr745.pd

Dudley, William C. 2018. "Important Choices for the Federal Reserve in the Years Ahead." Remarks at Lehman College, Bronx, New York, April 18. https://www.newyorkfed.org/newsevents/speeches/2018/dud180418a

Duffie, Darrell, and Arvind Krishnamurthy. 2016. "Pass-Through Efficiency in the Fed's New Monetary Policy Setting." In *Designing Resilient Monetary Policy Frameworks for the Future*. Kansas City: Federal Reserve Bank of Kansas City, pp. 21–101. https://www.kansascityfed.org/~/media/files/publicat/sympos/2016/2016shafik.pdf

Durden, Tyler. 2017. "40% of the Fed's Interest on Excess Reserves Is Paid to Foreign Banks." *ZeroHedge*, July 13. https://www.zerohedge.com/news/2017-07-13/40-feds-interest-excess-reserves-paid-foreign-banks

Dutkowsky, D. H., and David D. VanHoose. 2017. "Interest on Reserves, Regime Shifts, and Bank Behavior." *Journal of Economics and Business* 91: 1–15. https://www.sciencedirect.com/science/article/pii/S0148619516301047

Duval, Romain, Gee Hee Hong, and Yannick Timmer. 2017. "Financial Frictions and the Great Productivity Slowdown." IMF Working Paper WP/17/21, May. https://www.imf.org/~/media/Files/Publications/WP/2017/wp17129.ashx

Eggertsson, Gauti B., and Michael Woodford. 2003. "The Zero Bound on Interest Rates and Optimal Monetary Policy." *Brookings Papers on Economic Activity* (1): 139–233. https://www.brookings.edu/bpea-articles/the-zero-bound-on-interest-rates-and-optimal-monetary-policy/

Eggertsson, Gauti B., Ragnar E. Juelsrud, and Ella Getz Wold. 2017. "Are Negative Nominal Interest Rates Expansionary?" NBER Working Paper No. 24039, November. http://www.nber.org/papers/w24039

Ennis, Huberto, and Alexander Wolman. 2011. "Large Excess Reserves in the United States: A View from the Cross-Section of Banks." *International Journal of Central Banking* 11 (1): 251–89. http://www.ijcb.org/journal/ijcb15q1a8.pdf

Eubanks, Walter. 2002. "Proposals to Allow Federal Reserve Banks to Pay Interest on Reserve Balances: The Issues Behind the Legislation." *Congressional Research Service Report-RL30874*: 1–14. http://congressionalresearch.com/RL30874/document.php?study=Proposals+to+Allow+Federal+Reserve+Banks+to+Pay+Interest+on+Reserve+Balances+The+Issues+Behind+the+Legislation

Federal Reserve Bank of New York. 2017. "Statement Regarding the Publication of Overnight Treasury Repo Rates." Markets and Policy Implementation, May 24. https://www.newyorkfed.org/markets/opolicy/operating_policy_170524a

——————. 2018. "Statement Regarding the Publication of Overnight Treasury Repo Rates." Markets and Policy Implementation, April 3. https://www.newyorkfed.org/markets/opolicy/operating_policy_180403

Federal Reserve Bank of San Francisco. 2005. "What is Neutral Monetary Policy?" *Dr. Econ*, April. https://www.frbsf.org/education/publications/doctor-econ/2005/april/neutral-monetary-policy/

Feinman, Joshua N. 1993. "Reserve Requirements: History, Current Practice, and Potential Reform." *Federal Reserve Bulletin* (June): 569–89. https://www.federalreserve.gov/monetarypolicy/0693lead.pdf

Ferris, Erin, E. Syron, Soo Jeong Kim, and Bernd Schlusche. 2017. "Confidence Interval Projections of the Federal Reserve Balance Sheet and Income," FEDS Notes. Washington: Board of Governors of the Federal Reserve System, January 13, https://doi.org/10.17016/2380-7172.1875. https://www.federalreserve.gov/econresdata/notes/feds-notes/2017/confidence-interval-projections-of-the-federal-reserve-balance-sheet-and-income-20170113.html

Friedman, Milton. 1969. "The Optimum Quantity of Money." In idem, *The Optimum Quantity of Money and Other Essays*. Chicago: Aldine, pp. 1–50.

Furfine, Craig H. 2001. "Banks as Monitors of Other Banks: Evidence from the Overnight Federal Funds Market." *Journal of Business* 74 (1) (January): 33–57.

Gagnon, Joseph E. 2010. "Time for a Monetary Boost." *The Blog*, HuffPost, July 21. https://www.huffingtonpost.com/joseph-e-gagnon/time-for-a-monetary-boost_b_654944.html

_____. 2016. "Quantitative Easing: An Underappreciated Success." Peterson Institute for International Economics Policy Brief 16-4. https://piie.com/system/files/documents/pb16-4.pdf

Goodfriend, Marvin. 2002. "Interest on Reserves and Monetary Policy." Federal Reserve Bank of New York *Economic Policy Review* 8 (1): 77–84. https://www.newyorkfed.org/medialibrary/media/research/epr/02v08n1/0205good.pdf

Goodfriend, Marvin, and Monica Hargraves. 1983. "A Historical Assessment of the Rationales and Functions of Reserve Requirements." Federal Reserve Bank of Richmond *Economic Review* No. 69: 3–21. https://www.richmondfed.org/~/media/richmond fedorg/publications/.../wp83-1.pdf

Goodhart, Charles A. 2017. "The Optimal Size for Central Banks Balance Sheets." *Central Banking*, October 25. https://www.centralbanking .com/central-banks/governance/3311816/the-optimal-size-for -central-bank-balance-sheets

Garcia-de-Andoain, Carlos, Florian Heider, Marie Hoerova, and Simone Manganelli. 2016. "Lending-of-Last-Resort Is as Lending-of-Last-Resort Does: Central Bank Liquidity Provision and Inter-bank Market Functioning in the Euro Area." *Journal of Financial Intermediation* 28 (October): 32–47. https://www.sciencedirect .com/science/article/pii/S1042957316000103

Graham, Frank. 1930. *Exchange, Prices, and Production in Hyperinflation: Germany 1920–1923.* Princeton: Princeton University Press.

Greenlaw, David, James D. Hamilton, Ethan S. Harris, and Kenneth D. West. 2018. "A Skeptical View of the Impact of the Fed's Balance Sheet." Paper presented at the Chicago Booth School of Business U.S. Monetary Policy Forum, New York City, February 23. https:// research.chicagobooth.edu/-/media/research/igm/docs/2018-usmpf-report.pdf?la=en&hash=D8BE7A0F78D72A6762918282 D5A56A2E76349AED

Greenlaw, David, James D. Hamilton, Peter Hooper, and Frederic Mishkin. 2013. "The Federal Reserve's 'Fiscal Crunch' Trap." *Wall Street Journal*, March 7. https://www.wsj.com/articles/SB10001424 127887324338604578326031255455840

Greenwood, Robin, Samuel G. Hanson, and Jeremy C. Stein. 2016. "The Federal Reserve's Balance Sheet as a Financial-Stability Tool." In *Designing Monetary Policy Frameworks for the Future.* Kansas City: Federal

Reserve Bank of Kansas City, pp. 335–97. https://www.kansascityfed
.org/~/media/files/publicat/sympos/2016/2016steingreenwood
hanson.pdf?la=en

Haltom, Renee, and Robert Sharp. 2014. "The First Time the Fed
Bought GSE Debt." *Federal Reserve Bank of Richmond Economic
Brief*, April. https://www.richmondfed.org/~/media/richmondfed
org/publications/research/economic_brief/2014/pdf/eb_14-04.pdf

Hamilton, James D. 2017. "How the Federal Reserve Controls Interest
Rates." *Econbrowser*, March 27. http://econbrowser.com/archives
/2017/03/how-the-federal-reserve-controls-interest-rates

Hamilton, James D., and Jing Cynthia Wu. 2012. "The Effectiveness of
Alternative Monetary Policy Tools in a Zero Lower Bound Environment." *Journal of Money, Credit, and Banking* 44 (Supplement 1)
(February): 3–46. http://www.jstor.org.proxy-remote.galib.uga
.edu/stable/41336777

Hannan, Timothy. 1991. "Foundations of a Structure-Conduct-
Performance Paradigm in Banking." *Journal of Money, Credit, and Banking* 23 (1) (February): 68–84. http://www.jstor.org/stable/1992764

Harding, Robin. 2014. "US Quantitative Measures Worked in Defi-
ance of Theory." *Financial Times,* October 13. https://www.ft.com
/content/3b164d2e-4f03-11e4-9c88-00144feab7de

Heller, Robert. 2016. "How Congress Gutted the Fed's Capital Cof-
fers." *American Banker*, February 16. https://www.americanbanker.
com/opinion/how-congress-gutted-the-feds-capital-coffers

Higgins, Byron. 1977. "Interest Payments on Demand Deposits: Historical Evolution and the Current Controversy." Federal Reserve
Bank of Kansas City *Economic Review* July-August: 1–11. https://
www.kansascityfed.org/publicat/econrev/econrevarchive/1977
/3q77-j-a.pdf

Hoerva, Maria, and Cyrol Monnet. 2016. "Money Market Discipline
and Central Bank Lending." Unpublished working paper, May.
https://papers.ssrn.com/sol3/papers.cfm?abstract_id=2786501

Ihrig, Jane, Edward Kim, Ashish Kumbhat, Cindy Vojtech, and
Gretchen C. Weinbach. 2017. "How Have Banks been Manag-
ing the Composition of High-Quality Liquid Assets?" Federal
Reserve Board Finance and Economics Discussion Series 2017-12.
Washington: Board of Governors of the Federal Reserve System.
https://www.federalreserve.gov/econres/feds/files/2017092pap.pdf

Ireland, Peter N. 2018. "The Macroeconomic Effects of Interest on Reserves."*Macroeconomic Dynamics* 18 (6) (September): 1271–1312. https://www.cambridge.org/core/journals/macroeconomic -dynamics/article/macroeconomic-effects-of-interest-on-reserves /00983943FBE1469983FAC0C6E4BBAE40

Irwin, Neil. 2017. "Janet Yellen and the Case of the Missing Inflation." *New York Times*, June 14. https://www.nytimes.com/2017/06/14/ upshot/janet-yellen-and-the-case-of-the-missing-inflation.html

"Is the Federal Reserve Giving Banks a $12bn Subsidy?" 2017. *The Economist*, March 18. https://www.economist.com/news/ finance-and-economics/21718872-or-interest-fed-pays-them- vital-monetary-tool-benefits

Ito, Hiro. 2009. "Financial Repression." *The Princeton Encyclopedia of the World Economy*, v. 1. Princeton: Princeton University Press, pp. 430–33.

Jackson, Christopher, and Mathew Sim. 2013. "Recent Developments in the Sterling Overnight Money Market." Bank of England *Quarterly Bulletin* Q3: 223–32. https://www.bankofengland.co.uk/-/media /boe/files/quarterly-bulletin/2013/recent-developments-in-the -sterling-overnight-money-market.pdf?la=en&hash=F9CC590BFF BA5FBC9D478E3ABB32DC2765AAE081

Jobst, Andreas, and Huidan Lin. 2016. "Negative Interest Rate Policy (NIRP): Implications for Monetary Transmission and Bank Profit- ability in the Euro Area." IMF Working Paper WP/16/172, August. https://www.imf.org/external/pubs/ft/wp/2016/wp16172.pdf

Jokivuolle, Eso, Eero Tölö, and Matti Virén. 2015. "Do Banks' Over- night Borrowing Rates Lead Their CDS Price? Evidence from the Eurosystem." ECB Working Paper, No. 1809, June. https://www .ecb.europa.eu/pub/pdf/scpwps/ecbwp1809.en.pdf?fa414e8bb18 f09076c0186e9a02056f7

Jung, Taehun, Yuki Teranishi, and Tsutomo Watanabe. 2005. "Opti- mal Monetary Policy at the Zero-Interest-Rate Bound." *Journal of Money, Credit, and Banking* 37 (5) (October): 813–35. http://www .jstor.org/stable/3839148

Kahn, George A. 2010. "Monetary Policy under a Corridor Operating Framework." Federal Reserve Bank of Kansas City *Economic Review*, Fourth Quarter: 5–34. https://www.kansascityfed.org/ publicat/econrev/pdf/10q4Kahn.pdf

Keister, Todd. 2012. "Corridors and Floors in Monetary Policy." *Liberty Street Economics*, Federal Reserve Bank of New York, April 4. http://libertystreeteconomics.newyorkfed.org/2012/04/corridors -and-floors-in-monetary-policy.html

_____. 2018. "Interest on Reserves." Testimony before the Subcommittee on Monetary Policy and Trade, Committee on Financial Services, United States House of Representatives, May 17. https://financialservices.house.gov/uploadedfiles/hhrg-114-ba19- wstate-tkeister-20160517.pdf

Keating, Thomas, and Marco Macchiavelli. 2018. "Interest on Reserves and Arbitrage in Post-Crisis Money Markets." FEDS Notes, Washington: Board of Governors of the Federal Reserve System, March 1. https://doi.org/10.17016/2380-7172.2136

Keister, Todd, Antoine Martin, and James McAndrews. 2008. "Divorcing Money from Monetary Policy." Federal Reserve Bank of New York *Economic Policy Review*, September: 41–56. https://www.newyorkfed .org/research/epr/08v14n2/exesummary/exesum_keis.html

_____. 2015. "Floor Systems and the Friedman Rule: The Fiscal Arithmetic of Open Market Operations." Federal Reserve Bank of New York Staff Paper No. 754, December. https://www.newyorkfed .org/research/staff_reports/sr754.html

Klee, Elizabeth, Zeynep Senyuz, and Emre Yoldas. 2016. "Effects of Changing Monetary and Regulatory Policy on Overnight Money Markets." Finance and Economics Discussion Series 2016-084. Washington: Board of Governors of the Federal Reserve System. https://doi.org/10.17016/FEDS.2016.084

Klein, Michael A. 1971. "A Theory of the Banking Firm." *Journal of Money, Credit and Banking* 3 (2) (May): 205–18. http://www.jstor .org/stable/1991279

Kohn, Donald. 2005. "Regulatory Relief," Testimony before the Subcommittee on Financial Institutions and Consumer Credit, Committee on Financial Services, U.S. House of Representatives, June 9. https:// www.federalreserve.gov/boarddocs/testimony/2005/20050609/ default.htm

_____. 2009. "Policy Challenges for the Federal Reserve." Speech at the Kellogg School of Management, Northwestern University, Evanston, Illinois, November 16. https://www.federalreserve.gov/ newsevents/speech/kohn20091116a.htm

Koning, J. P. 2016. "Cashing Up the System" *Moneyness* (Blog), January 1. http://jpkoning.blogspot.com/2015/01/cashing-up-system.html

Kotok, David. 2016. "LCR: Is the Fed's Balance Sheet Too Small." Cumberland Advisors Market Commentary, June 9. http://www .cumber.com/lcr-is-the-fedas-balance-sheet-too-small/

Kravis, Marie-Josée. 2017. "The Great Productivity Slowdown." *Wall Street Journal*, May 4. https://www.wsj.com/articles/the-great-productivity -slowdown-1493939350

Kroeger, Alexander, and Asani Sarkar. 2016. "Monetary Policy Transmission before and after the Crisis." *Liberty Street Economics*, June 29. http://libertystreeteconomics.newyorkfed.org/2016/06/monetary -policy-transmission-before-and-after-the-crisis.html

Krugman, Paul. 2014. "Nobody Could Have Predicted, Monetary Edition." *New York Times*, March 19. https://krugman.blogs .nytimes.com/2014/03/19/nobody-could-have-predicted-monetary -edition/

Laubach, Thomas, and John C. Williams. 2015. "Measuring the Natural Rate of Interest Redux." Federal Reserve Bank of San Francisco Working Paper 2015–16. http://www.frbsf.org/ economic-research/publications/working-papers/wp2015-16.pdf

Laurent, Robert, and Larry Mote. 1985. "Some Neglected Problems in Paying Interest on Reserves." Working paper, Federal Reserve Bank of Chicago.

Levine, Ross. 1997. "Financial Development and Economic Growth: Views and Agenda." *Journal of Economic Literature* 35 (2), June: 688–726. https://www.jstor.org/stable/2729790

Lipscomb, Laura, Antoine Martin, and Heather Wiggins. 2017. "Why Pay Interest on Excess Reserve Balances?" *Liberty Street Economics*, September 27. http://libertystreeteconomics.newyorkfed.org/2017 /09/why-pay-interest-on-excess-reserve-balances.html

Logan, Lorie K. 2018. "Implementing Monetary Policy: Perspective from the Open Market Trading Desk." Remarks before the Money Marketeers of New York University, New York City, May 18. https://www.newyorkfed.org/newsevents/speeches/2017/ log170518

"Market Rate Rise May Thwart Fed's Balance Sheet Plan." 2018. *New York Times*, June 27. https://www.nytimes.com/reuters/2018 /06/27/business/27reuters-usa-fed-ioer-analysis.html

Martin, Antoine, James McAndrews, and David Skeie. 2013. "Bank Lending in Times of Large Bank Reserves," Federal Reserve Bank of New York Staff Report No. 497, June. https://www.newyorkfed.org/research/staff_reports/sr497.html

McCulloch, J. Huston. 2018. "Normalizing Monetary Policy." *Cato Journal*, forthcoming.

McKinnon, Ronald. 2011. "The Return of Stagflation." *Wall Street Journal*, May 24. https://www.wsj.com/articles/SB10001424052702304066504576341211971664684

Meltzer, Allan H. 2003. *A History of the Federal Reserve, vol. 1: 1913–1951.* Chicago: University of Chicago Press.

Merler, Silvia. 2018. "The Financial Side of the Productivity Slowdown." *Bruegel.org*, January 22. http://bruegel.org/2018/01/the-financial-side-of-the-productivity-slowdown/

Meyer, Laurence. 2000. "Payment of Interest on Reserves and Fed Surplus." Testimony before the Committee on Banking and Financial Services, U.S. House of Representatives, May 3. https://www.federalreserve.gov/boarddocs/testimony/2000/20000503.htm

Mora, Nada. 2014. "The Weakened Transmission of Monetary Policy to Consumer Loan Rates." Federal Reserve Bank of Kansas City *Economic Review* Q1: 1–26. http://www.kansascityfed.org/publicat/econrev/pdf/14q1Mora.pdf

Nelson, Bill. 2018. "A Former Fed Insider Explains the Internal Debate over QE3." *FTAlphaville*, February 16. https://ftalphaville.ft.com/2018/02/16/2198845/guest-post-a-former-fed-insider-explains-the-internal-debate-over-qe3/

Noizet, Julien. 2016. "Misunderstanding the Net Interest Margin." *Alt-M*, June 1. https://www.alt-m.org/2016/06/01/misunderstanding-the-net-interest-margin/

Norges Bank. 2011. "Background for the System for Managing Bank Reserves in Norway," June 20. https://www.norges-bank.no/en/Liquidity-and-markets/The-liquidity-management-system/The-management-of-bank-reserves-The-system-in-Norway/Background-system-managing-bank-reserves/.

_____. 2014. "Banks' Assessment of Norges Bank's Liquidity Management System." Norges Bank Papers No. 4. https://www.norges-bank.no/contentassets/.../norges_bank_papers_2014_4.pdf

Nunes, Marcus. 2014. "Identifying' the Stance of Monetary Policy." *Historinhas*, March 1. https://thefaintofheart.wordpress.com/2014/03/01/identifying-the-stance-of-monetary-policy/

Ogawa, Kazuo. 2007. "Why Commercial Banks Held Excess Reserves: The Japanese Experience of the Late 1990s." *Journal of Money, Credit, and Banking* 39 (1) (February): 241–57. http://www.jstor.org/stable/4123077

Orphanides, Athanasios. 2004. "Monetary Policy in Deflation: The Liquidity Trap in History and Practice." *North American Journal of Economics and Finance* 15 (1) (March): 101–24. https://www.sciencedirect.com/science/article/abs/pii/S1062940803000524

Papadia, Francesco. 2014. "Where Could ECB Interest Rates Go?" *Money Matters: Perspectives on Monetary Policy*, May 20. http://moneymatters-monetarypolicy.eu/where-could-ecb-interest-rates-go/

Pérignon, Christophe, David Thesmar, and Guillaume Villemey. 2018. "Wholesale Funding Dry-Ups." *Journal of Finance*, forthcoming. http://journal.afajof.org/article/wholesale-funding-dry-ups/

Petrou, Karen. 2016. "Why Ending IOER Isn't Easy." *The Vault*, Federal Financial Analytics, December 16. http://www.fedfin.com/blog/2265-karen-petrou-on-why-ending-ioer-isn-t-easy

Phelps, Edmund. 1973. "Inflation in the Theory of Public Finance." *Swedish Journal of Economics* 75 (1) (March): 67–82. http://www.jstor.org/stable/3439275

Plosser, Charles. 2017. "The Risks of a Fed Balance Sheet Unconstrained by Monetary Policy." Hoover Institution Economics Working Paper 17102, May 4. https://www.hoover.org/sites/default/files/research/docs/17102-plosser.pdf

Pozsar, Zoltan. 2016. "What Excess Reserves?" *Global Money Notes #5*, Credit Suisse, April 13. https://research-doc.credit-suisse.com/docView?language=ENG&format=PDF&document_id=1060091811&source_id=emcmt&serialid=6kOK62k2brRsDf2wXpet09oFz7BQArYk93VobPupfmk=

Potter, Simon. 2015. "Money Markets and Monetary Policy Normalization." Speech at the Money Marketeers of New York University. https://www.newyorkfed.org/newsevents/speeches/2015/pot150415.html

Powell, Jerome H. 2017. "Thoughts on the Normalization of Monetary Policy." Speech at the Economic Club of New York,

New York City, June 1. https://www.federalreserve.gov/news events/speech/powell20170601a.htm

Prague, Shawn. 2017. "Below Trend: the U.S. Productivity Slowdown Since the Great Recession." Bureau of Labor Statistics *Beyond the Numbers* 6 (2): January. https://www.bls.gov/opub/btn/volume-6 /below-trend-the-us-productivity-slowdown-since-the-great -recession.htm

Redmond, Michael, and Willem Van Zandweghe. 2016. "The Lasting Damage from the Financial Crisis to U.S. Productivity." Federal Reserve Bank of Kansas City *Economic Review*, First Quarter: 39–64. https://www.kansascityfed.org/publicat/econrev /.../1q16redmondvanzandweghe.pdf

Regulation D: Reserve Requirements for Depository Institutions. 2015. "Rules and Regulations." *Federal Register 80*, No. 119, June 22: 35567. https://www.gpo.gov/fdsys/pkg/FR-2015-06-22 /pdf/2015-15238.pdf

Reifschneider, David, and John C. Williams. 2000. "Three Lessons for Monetary Policy in a Low-Inflation Era." *Journal of Money, Credit, and Banking* 32 (4, Part 2) (November): 936–66. http://www.jstor .org/stable/2601151

Reinhart, Carmen M., and Kenneth S. Rogoff. 2009. "The Aftermath of Financial Crises." *American Economic Review* 99 (2) (May): 466–72. http://www.jstor.org/stable/pdf/25592442.pdf?refreqid=excelsior %3A204ebca585eb8f70e710a2cf08872a1f

Reis, Ricardo. 2016. "Funding Quantitative Easing to Target Inflation." In *Designing Monetary Policy Frameworks for the Future*. Kansas City: Federal Reserve Bank of Kansas City, pp. 423–78. https://www.kansascityfed .org/~/media/files/publicat/sympos/2016/2016reis.pdf?la=en

Richter, Wolf. 2018. "The Fed Paid Banks $30 Billion on 'Excess Reserves' for 2017." *Business Insider*, January 11. http://www .businessinsider.com/fed-paid-banks-30-billion-on-excess-reserves -for-2017-2018-1

Robb, Gregg. 2012. "One Fed Tool that Gives Wall Street Heartburn." *MarketWatch*, July 25. https://www.marketwatch.com/story/one- fed-tool-that-gives-wall-street-heartburn-2012-07-25

Rochet, Jean-Charles, and Jean Tirole. 1996. "Interbank Lending and Systemic Risk." *Journal of Money, Credit, and Banking* 28 (4) (November): 733–62. http://www.jstor.org/stable/2077918

Roubini, Nouriel, and Xavier Sala-i-Martin. 1992. "Financial Repression and Economic Growth." *Journal of Development Economics* 39 (1) (July): 5–30. https://www.sciencedirect.com/science/article/pii/030438789290055E

Sargent, Thomas, and Neil Wallace. 1985. "Interest on Reserves." *Journal of Monetary Economics* 15 (3) (May): 259–90. https://www.sciencedirect.com/science/article/pii/0304393285900169

Schmitt-Grohé, Stephanie, and Martín Uribe. 2004 "Optimal Fiscal and Monetary Policy under Sticky Prices." *Journal of Economic Theory* 114 (2) (February): 198–230. https://www.sciencedirect.com/science/article/pii/S002205310300111X

Selgin, George. 2016. "New York's Bank: The National Monetary Commission and the Founding of the Fed." Cato Institute *Policy Analysis* No. 793, June 2016. https://object.cato.org/sites/cato.org/files/pubs/pdf/pa-793.pdf

————. 2017a. "A Monetary Policy Primer, Part 9: Monetary Control, Now." *Alt-M*, January 10. https://www.alt-m.org/2017/01/10/monetary-policy-primer-part-9-monetary-control-now/

————. 2017b. "Interest on Reserves: A Secret Fiscal Weapon We're Better Off Without." *Alt-M*, January 25. https://www.alt-m.org/2017/01/25/interest-on-reserves-a-secret-fiscal-weapon-were-better-off-without/

————. 2018a. "New Zealand's Floor System Experience." *Alt-M*, March 8. https://www.alt-m.org/2018/03/08/new-zealands-floor-system-experience/

————. 2018b. "Dudley's Defense of the Fed's Floor System." *Alt-M*, May 3. https://www.alt-m.org/2018/05/03/dudleys-defense-of-the-feds-floor-system/

Sellin, Peter, and Per Åsberg. 2014. "The Riksbank's Operational Framework for the Implementation of Monetary Policy—a Review." *Riksbank Studies*, March 20. www.riksbank.se/Documents/Rapporter/Riksbanksstudie/2014/rap_riksbanksstudie_140326_eng.pdf

Sumner, Scott. 2011. "Re-Targeting the Fed." *National Affairs* 9 (Fall): 79–96. https://www.nationalaffairs.com/publications/detail/re-targeting-the-fed

————. 2013. "Interest Rates are Always and Everywhere a Horrible Guide to the Stance of Monetary Policy." *TheMoneyIllusion*, April 18.

http://www.themoneyillusion.com/interest-rates-are-always-and
-everywhere-a-horrible-guide-to-the-stance-of-monetary-policy/

_____. 2017. "Time to Abolish Interest on Reserves." *TheMoney-Illusion*, March 14. http://www.themoneyillusion.com/?p=32380

Taylor, John B. 1993. "Discretion versus Policy Rules in Practice." *Carnegie-Rochester Conference Series on Public Policy* 39: 195–214. https://www.sciencedirect.com/science/article/pii/016722319390009L

_____. 2009. *Getting Off Track: How Government Actions and Interventions Caused, Prolonged, and Worsened the Financial Crisis.* Stanford, CA: Hoover Institution Press.

Thornton, Daniel L. 2015. "Requiem for QE." Cato Institute *Policy Analysis* No. 783, November. https://object.cato.org/sites/cato.org/files/pubs/pdf/pa783_1.pdf

_____. 2017. "Effectiveness of QE: An Assessment of Event-Study Evidence." *Journal of Macroeconomics* 52 (June): 56–74. https://www.sciencedirect.com/science/article/pii/S0164070417300939

United States, Government Accountability Office. 2017. "Federal Reserve System: Potential Implications of Modifying the Capital Surplus Account and Stock Ownership Requirement." GAO-17-243, February 24. https://www.gao.gov/products/GAO-17-243

van den End, Jan Willem. 2017. "Applying Complexity Theory to Interest Rates: Evidence of Critical Transitions in the Euro Area." DNB Working Paper No. 567, September. https://www.dnb.nl/en/binaries/Working%20Paper%20No%2E%20567_tcm47-362742.pdf

Wall, Larry D. 2015. "Financing the Fed's Balance Sheet: Implications for the Treasury." *Notes from the Vault.* Federal Reserve Bank of Atlanta, Center for Financial Innovation and Stability, December. https://www.frbatlanta.org/cenfis/publications/notesfromthevault/1512.aspx

_____. 2017. "Interest on Reserves." *Notes from the Vault*, Federal Reserve Bank of Atlanta, February. https://www.frbatlanta.org/cenfis/publications/notesfromthevault/02-interest-on-reserves-2017-02-27.aspx

Walsh, Carl E. 1984. "Optimal Taxation by the Monetary Authority." NBER Working Paper No. 1375. June. www.nber.org/papers/w1375

Walter, John R., and Renee Courtois. 2009. "The Effect of Interest on Reserves on Monetary Policy." Federal Reserve Bank of

Richmond *Economic Brief* EB09-12, December. https://www
.richmondfed.org/-/media/richmondfedorg/publications/
research/economic_brief/2009/pdf/eb_09-12.pdf

Weiner, Stuart. 1985. "Payment of Interest on Reserves." Federal Reserve
Bank of Kansas City *Economic Review*, January: 16–31. https://www
.kansascityfed.org/gRQLP/cNmOn/VZcRZ/.../1985/1q85wein.pdf

Wen, Yi. 2014. "Evaluating Unconventional Monetary Policies—Why
Aren't They More Effective?" Federal Reserve Bank of St. Louis
Working Paper 2013-028B, January. https://research.stlouisfed
.org/wp/2013/2013-028.pdf

Whitesell, William. 2006. "Interest Rate Corridors and Reserves."
Journal of Monetary Economics 53 (6) (September): 1177–95. https://
www.sciencedirect.com/science/article/pii/S0304393206000572

Williams, John C. 2012. "Monetary Policy, Money, and Inflation."
FRBSF *Economic Letter*, July 9. https://www.frbsf.org/economic
-research/publications/economic-letter/2012/july/monetary
-policy-money-inflation/el2012-21.pdf

Wilkinson, Jim, and Jon Christensson. 2011. "Can the Supply of Small
Business Loans Be Increased?" Federal Reserve Bank of Kansas City
Economic Review, April: 35–57. www.kansascityfed.org/UQNkZ/
LmaPZ/YaOcZ/.../11q2wilkinson-christensson.pdf

Williamson, Stephen D. 2012. Liquidity, Monetary Policy, and the
Financial Crisis: A New Monetarist Approach." *American Economic
Review* 102 (6) (October): 2570–2605. http://www.jstor.org/
stable/41724665

_____. 2016. "Interest Rate Control Is More Complicated
Than You Thought." *Regional Economist*, Federal Reserve Bank
of St. Louis, April. https://www.stlouisfed.org/publications/
regional-economist/april-2016/interest-rate-control-is-more-
complicated-than-you-thought

_____. 2017a. "Balance Sheet Blues." *New Monetarist Economics*,
February. http://newmonetarism.blogspot.com/2017/02/balance-
sheet-blues.html

_____. 2017b. "Quantitative Easing: How Well Does This Tool
Work?" *Regional Economist*, Federal Reserve Bank of St. Louis,
Third Quarter. https://www.stlouisfed.org/publications/regional
-economist/third-quarter-2017/quantitative-easing-how-well
-does-this-tool-work

Winters, Bill. 2012. "Review of the Bank of England's Framework for Providing Liquidity to the Banking System." Report Presented to the Court of the Bank of England. www.bankofengland.co.uk/-/media/boe/files/news/2012/november/the-banks-framework-for-providing-liquidity-

Wolf, Martin, 2014. "Only the Ignorant Live in Fear of Hyperinflation." *Financial Times*, April 10. https://www.ft.com/content/46a1ce84-bf2a-11e3-a4af-00144feabdc0

Woodford, Michael. 2012. "Methods of Policy Accommodation at the Interest-Rate Lower Bound." Unpublished manuscript, Columbia University, September 16. https://www.kansascityfed.org/publicat/sympos/2012/mw.pdf

Wright, Jonathan H. 2012. "What Does Monetary Policy Do to Long-Term Interest Rates at the Zero Lower Bound?" *Economic Journal* 122 (564) (November): F447–F466. http://www.jstor.org.proxy-remote.galib.uga.edu/stable/23324230

Yellen, Janet. 2015. "The Economic Outlook and Monetary Policy." Remarks at the Economic Club of Washington, Washington, D.C., December 2. https://www.federalreserve.gov/newsevents/speech/files/yellen20151202a.pdf

——————. 2016. "The Federal Reserve's Monetary Policy Toolkit: Past, Present, and Future." Remarks delivered at the Federal Reserve Bank of Kansas City symposium "Designing Resilient Monetary Policy Frameworks for the Future." Jackson Hole, Wyoming, August 26. https://www.federalreserve.gov/newsevents/speech/yellen20160826a.pdf

——————. 2017a. "Transcript of Chair Yellen's Press Conference." Board of Governors of the Federal Reserve System, June 14. https://www.federalreserve.gov/mediacenter/files/FOMCpresconf20170614.pdf

——————. 2017b. "Semiannual Monetary Policy Report to the Congress." Testimony before the Committee on Financial Services, U.S. House of Representatives, July 12. https://www.federalreserve.gov/newsevents/testimony/yellen20170712a.htm

Zumbrun, Josh. 2016. "Four Legal Questions the Fed Would Face If It Decided to Go Negative." *Wall Street Journal*, February 10. https://blogs.wsj.com/economics/2016/02/10/four-legal-questions-the-fed-would-face-if-it-decided-to-go-negative/

INDEX

Note: Page numbers followed by f and n indicate figures and notes, respectively.

ABOUT THE AUTHOR

George Selgin directs the Cato's Institute's Center for Monetary and Financial Alternatives and is Professor Emeritus of Economics at the University of Georgia. His other books include *The Theory of Free Banking*, *Bank Deregulation and Monetary Order*, *Good Money*, and *Money: Free and Unfree*.

ABOUT THE CATO INSTITUTE
AND ITS CENTER FOR MONETARY
AND FINANCIAL ALTERNATIVES

Founded in 1977, the Cato Institute is a public policy research foundation dedicated to broadening the parameters of policy debate to allow consideration of more options that are consistent with the principles of limited government, individual liberty, and peace.

The Institute is named for *Cato's Letters*, libertarian pamphlets that were widely read in the American Colonies in the early 18th century and played a major role in laying the philosophical foundation for the American Revolution.

The Cato Institute undertakes an extensive publications program on the complete spectrum of policy issues. Books, monographs, and shorter studies are commissioned to examine the federal budget, Social Security, regulation, military spending, international trade, and myriad other issues. Major policy conferences are held throughout the year.

The Cato Institute's Center for Monetary and Financial Alternatives was founded in 2014 to assess the shortcomings of existing monetary and financial regulatory arrangements, and to discover and promote more stable and efficient alternatives.

In order to maintain its independence, the Cato Institute accepts no government funding. Contributions are received from foundations, corporations, and individuals, and other revenue is generated from the sale of publications. The Institute is a non-profit, tax-exempt, educational foundation under Section 501(c)3 of the Internal Revenue Code.

CATO INSTITUTE
1000 Massachusetts Avenue, N.W.
Washington, D.C. 20001
www.cato.org

CPSIA information can be obtained
at www.ICGtesting.com
Printed in the USA
LVHW090725030121
675430LV00011BA/2198